Dedicated to George Floyd

*and Eagles co-founders
Kenny Johnson and Joe Roberts*

John Wareham is a coach and
counselor to serious upward
strivers, from celebrated
corporate chiefs to maximum
security prison inmates.
John established the not-for-profit
Eagles Circle Foundation, Inc. to
identify and develop leaders
from within the prison system.
Since 1995, working as an unpaid
volunteer, he created
and ran highly successful Eagles
inmate development programs
inside New York's toughest prisons,
including Rikers Island, the
world's largest penal colony.

www.eaglegather.org
www.johnwareham.com

PRAISE FOR WAREHAM'S WORK

"**Compelling** . . . Wareham shares a riveting journey into the mind, heart and soul . . . if ever there was a master key to the mental penitentiary, this is it." **—Jess D. Maghan**
professor emeritus, criminal justice, University of Illinois,
former director of training New York City
Police and Corrections Departments.

"**Invigorating** . . . bold ideas, and an almost cocky tone combine with charm, and edgy, intricate logic to create a book that will result in a fresh and energized perspective." **—Library Journal**

"**Inspired** . . . philosophically savvy." **—Kirkus Reviews**

"**Powerful** . . . Wareham's unusual sociological premise, real life examples and highly readable format will appeal to those seeking to change their lives." **—Publishers Weekly**

"**Wise.** . . uniquely insightful." **—Booklist, American Library**

"**Eye-opening** . . . Wareham offers up a profound and creative thesis of transforming a specious sense of personal autonomy into a pure sense of freedom. Ironically, the self-elucidating nature of Wareham's journey into the heart and soul of Riker's Island becomes even more transparent in light of the spurious greed among the current cast of corporate crooks."

—The Keepers' Voice

"**Profound** . . . Wareham's psychological understanding and nicely tuned intuition show how to give up the life of fantasy and achieve our greatest satisfactions.' **—Leo Madow, M.D.**
Psychiatrist and author of Anger and Love.

"**Transformational** . . . the variety of content, and clear, engaging presentation is outstanding; it is a stunning complex of relevant experiential and solid evidential-based material that should shake many on both sides of the fence to the core." **—Tony Taylor**
Professor Emeritus of psychology,
Victoria University of Wellington, New Zealand.

"**Life-changing**—passionate and honest, ennobling and enriching."

—Charles DeFanti

Professor Emeritus, Kean University

Thanks to my always inspiring Eagles co-founders and Rikers Island colleagues, Kenny Johnson and Joe Roberts, both of whom passed all too early from this life. To everyone at the Osborne Association who drew me into teaching on Rikers Island. To Hassan Gale, who, with Marvin Gallaway, brought the Eagles program to Wallkill and Downstate prisons. To Eagles graduates and teachers Talib McFadden, Jason Rodriguez, Dwayne Speight and Richard Habersham. To Downstate librarian Juanita Carmichael, who championed the program, and to Neville Wells, who worked so hard to make it the success it became. To Brian O'Dea who often drove a thousand miles to help run our prison programs. To Anthony 'Lucky' Hopkins, Bernard Mindich, John Chaney and Omar Tsourtakis who inspired Eagles graduates. Special thanks to every inmate who ever enrolled in the program—and thereby taught me so much about the forces that lead to incarceration, and the equally powerful forces that lead to authentic freedom. To Eagles supporters Dr. Jess Maghan, Sister Teresa Donworth, Mike and Cynthia Gibbons, Jim Adrian, and Shell and Susan Evans. To Huan Zhang who pressed me to create the podcast series that in turn gave birth to this book. To Craig Rubano and Madeleine Collinge whose help with that adaptation was invaluable. To Dean Wareham, Mark Nadler, Carmel McGlone and Beth Manson whose words of encouragement were more inspiring than they likely realize. And, of course, my most special thanks to my wife and lifetime guardian angel, Margaret.

*"Be thine own palace
or the world's thy jail."*

John Donne (1572-1631)
poet, scholar, soldier, cleric

*"Don't be shocked when I say that I was
in prison—some of you are still in prison!"*

Malcolm X (1925-1965)
Civil rights pioneer. From speech to Cory Methodist Church,
Cleveland, Ohio, April 3, 1964.

*"No matter what side of the wall we're
on, the world's biggest prison
is between the ears."*

Hassan Gale
Prison reformer, Eagles program director.
From speech to 'at-risk' youth, Harlem, 2020

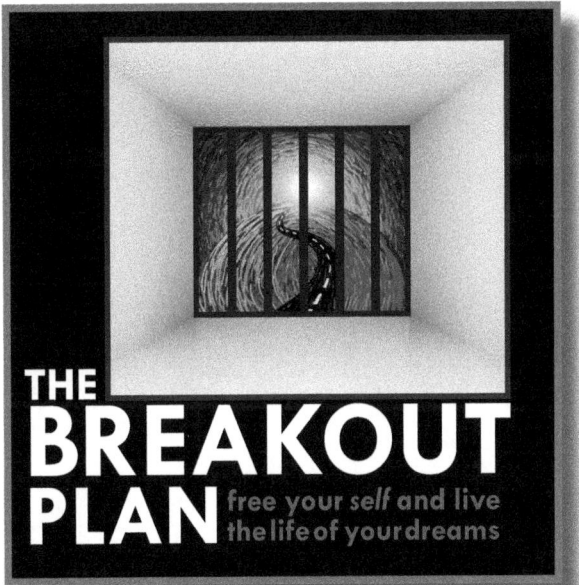

THE
BREAKOUT
PLAN

free your *self* and live
the life of your dreams

JOHN WAREHAM

Contents

The Parable of the Golden Eagle

by Anthony de Mello

A man found an eagle's egg and put in the nest of a backyard hen. The eaglet hatched with the brood of chicks and grew up with them.

He thought he was a backyard chicken, so all his life the eagle did what the backyard chickens did.

He clucked and cackled and scratched the earth for worms and insects. And he would thrash his wings and fly a few feet into the air.

Years passed and the eagle grew very old. One day he saw a magnificent bird far above him in the cloudless sky. It glided in graceful majesty among the powerful wind currents, with scarcely a beat of its strong golden wings.

The old eagle looked up in awe. "Who is that?" he asked.

"That's the eagle, the king of the birds," said his neighbor. "He belongs to the sky. We belong to the earth—we're chickens."

And so the eagle lived and died a chicken.

Breakout Invitation

What You're In For, by Hassan Gale

I've had the misfortune of doing serious time in some of New York's most notorious prisons.

That's where I met John Wareham. I heard about him from a good friend who was also a former prisoner. He spoke so highly of John that I was able to persuade an administrator to invite him in and share the program he created for prisoners on Rikers Island, at that time the world's largest penal colony. It was also one of the most violent. John's approach is not only entirely new, but also profound and powerful. Lives and perspectives, including my own, were constructively challenged. His approach makes it extremely difficult, if not impossible, to ignore stranglehold, that mental prisons can have on our lives. Where these prisons come from, how they survive, and the keys needed to escape them are skillfully explained and graphically exposed.

When I was released twelve years ago, John invited me to become an Eagles instructor. Now I run those programs and train potential facilitators. So, maybe we'll meet up one day. Meantime, you can catch me on our podcasts, and, right now, this little book will be your friend and guide. *Peace* . . . §

What's Happening?

The Life-Altering 4-Walls Model

Well, hello there. I'm John Wareham, creator of The Breakout Plan.

Since you've found us, I'm thinking that maybe you've recently been released from one of our so-called correctional facilities. Or maybe you're still in one. Or maybe, people are telling you that unless things change, you're in danger or winding up there.

Doesn't matter.

Some of our greatest citizens wind up in prison.

And there are no mistakes in life, just lessons.

What does matter is that bad things seem to keep happening to you.

And, maybe, since you're listening, you're thinking there's got to be a better way. Well there is! And by tuning in today, you're already on your way.

Race and Justice

First up, I just want to say that given the massive protests I think we can agree that the killing of George Floyd in police custody turned out to be an historic event.

For sure it created, at least within this new generation of protestors, a new intolerance for police brutality and racialized institutional bias.

I was confronted with precisely those problems in my very first class to Rikers Island inmates.

Only three of 30 inmates were white. But everyone had been hurt by racism, and everyone wanted to talk about it.

And so, to the alarm of officialdom, we did just that.

Nothing was off the table. Our discussions were frank, forthright, candid—and never politically correct. They generated heat and, finally, a healing light for everyone—especially me.

With bigotry no longer a distraction, we created a life-altering, laser-focused program, centered on showing how to get out of jail and create the life you know you deserve. Racism and institutional bias deserve special treatment, so we've added an epilogue, which you can go straight to at any point.

Here We Go Then

Let's begin with lines delivered to the Downstate class by Eagles graduate, Sheldon, describing how he felt in the moment of moment of his arrest.

> *Who am I?*
> *What have I done?*
> *I can't believe I did that.*
> *What have I become?*
> *Why are those guys oozing red?*
> *That one looks just like he's dead.*
> *They're starin' at me, everyone.*
> *Wherever did I get this gun?*

Powerful and tragic, right? The *Poets and Writers* organization supported publication of this poem in our book, *How to Survive a Bullet to the Heart—uncensored confessions of maximum security inmates*. It's on Amazon if you'd like to check it out.

Sheldon's Question—'wherever did I get this gun'—demands a truthful answer. And, even though I've been warned by law enforcement officials not to disclose it, that's what I'll be sharing with you in a moment.

Right now, though, let me reveal a secret.

Winning Parole

Police officers, judges, and parole boards are conflicted.

They want to be admired as respected, fair, and forgiving citizens. So, they're always on the lookout for someone to release.

BUT they also live in fear of releasing any lawbreaker who then screws up and returns to jail.

Their deep dread is that if they let *you* go, you'll reoffend and bring shame down upon *them*.

> *So the first thing they look for is a reason to keep you locked up.*

Your needs mean nothing, and your remorse and rehabilitation is only of interest if seems to be lacking.

But, and listen carefully now, a savvy parole board also appreciates that:

> *You're infinitely less likely to reoffend if you truly know <u>why</u> you offended in the first place.*

Once you truly know that, your head will be clearer, your heart lighter, and you'll become confident of your ability to create a whole new life, and you'll be inspired to achieve just that.

> *So, what they want to hear—and they want to hear it from your lips—is a deep and authentic understanding of why you committed your crime.*

Sounds easy, right? But here's the crocodile in the bathtub.

Even as you're listening to me right now, I'm betting that you already think that you know why you broke the law.

But, with the greatest respect, you do *not*.

And until you do, you'll likely remain within the clutches of the law.

And, as we'll see in a moment, *you* won't let *yourself* out of prison either.

All of which brings us to the Breakout Plan.

Wrap your head and your heart around these startling ideas, and, even if you're inside a steel hotel right now, you'll become a free citizen forever.

Not So Simple

The bad news is that the Breakout Plan is not a simple plan.

The good news is that it distills the world's biggest life-altering ideas into a truly life-changing model.

We call it the 4-Walls Model. And once you get it, you'll never forget it.

Stay the course and it will become unforgettable.

Un-for-get-able.

That's why the recidivism rate for Eagles graduates is in the single digits, and in one ten-year stint it was nil.

Those guys graduated because they stayed the course. And they stayed because they were savvy and intellectually curious.

And since you've gone to the trouble of signing in, I'm assuming that you are, too.

So hang in there.

At the journey's end, the message will be, well, unforgettable.

Just to be clear, the Eagles Circle Foundation is unaligned to any religion or *ism*. Our only goal is to help you create the life you know in your heart you deserve.

But from time to time we all need a little help with that.

So, first, we'll show why things go wrong and leave you feeling that you've been trapped in a life you didn't truly choose—and, as I kind of said already, the reasons for that are *not* what you think!

Next, we'll show how to release the inner genie you have bottled up inside you, and then we'll help you to create the life that we both know you were meant to live.

THE BIG IDEA

So, here's the over-arching, life-altering concept—the all-embracing big idea:

All prisons are mental prisons.

And every mental prison has four walls, a door, a lock, and a key.

They lock from the inside and you hold the key—so only you can let yourself out.

We call this the 4-Walls Model. This is a vital concept. You will keep winding up back in prison until you truly understand why you're in it.

- The first wall is home to a *snake.*
- The second houses a *gremlin.*
- A merciless lady—a *witch*, actually—awaits you inside the third wall.
- And a *zombie* is staggering inside the fourth wall.

In our next sessions we'll open the first three walls and reveal the snake, the gremlin, and the witch.

Right now, because he stymies our ability to fully understand how these tormentors trap us in mental prisons, we're gonna stir up the zombie inside the fourth wall.

It's the wall some people never get to see, and, for those who do, it mostly appears too late in life to do anything about it.

It's the wall that every official who ever wagged a finger in your face knows nothing about.

It's the wall that justice and prison officials warned me not to talk about.

And, it's the wall that even you may find hard to acknowledge, but which your heart will soon enough tell you exists.

So, stay with me now, 'cos here we go—

WRONG CHOICES?

For openers, I'm willing to bet that a bunch of irate parents and teachers, and priests and policemen, scolded you because, they said:

> *You keep on making the wrong choices. You just gotta learn to think before you act. But you're a slow learner. And always headed in the wrong direction.*

Well, it seems that those unhappy and hurtful homilies claim a permanent place in the brain cells.

I say that because 143 of the guys who enrolled in our prison class also completed an open ended sentence: *I'm in jail because . . .*

Only four of them showed any real understanding of why they did what they did:

- Nine (6%) said they were fools or idiots.
- One in 20 (5%) said doing drugs or selling drugs landed them inside.
- Ten (7%) blamed other people.

But get this now:

- 52—just over a third—said, 'I made the wrong choices.'
- 84—just short of 60% said the same thing another way: I made a mistake, or I simply lost control of my emotions and committed a crime.

Like I said, just about nobody truly knew what it was in

their hearts and minds that drove the criminal behavior that landed them in jail.

Tapping Into the Heart

On condition that I add the teaching of poetry to the Eagles classes, the Poets and Writers organization offered to help us publish a book of inmate poems. So my Downstate guys opened their hearts and wrote a bunch of great stuff about how they felt in the moment of their crime. Here's a sampling, first from William—note his opening line:

> I had to've been out of my mind.
> The goal was merely to reprimand,
> instead Death played trumps with a ghastly hand.
> That night I could not sleep
>> or count the time.
> Next day you could see in my eye,
>> that moment of my crime.

Rudy, immediately after firing his weapon and not knowing which way to run, tells a similar story—this time note the last line:

> Untold faces, cold stares,
>> reluctant glares,
>> stick to you like glue.
> Temperamental escalator,
>> up and down,
>> run or freeze
>> which ride is true?
> In the moment of my crime,
>> I swear I shoulda knew.

So there it is again: I had to've been out of my mind, and I swear I shoulda knew! Really? And think back to Sheldon's question: Wherever did I get this gun?

Here's just the man to tell you . . .

The Wall of the Zombie

He's Not Dead Yet—Just Sleeping

The late great social reformer Malcolm X offered a heartfelt confession with a haunting message:

> *I did many things that I'm sorry for now. I was a zombie then . . . I was hypnotized, pointed in a certain direction and told to march. Well, I guess a man's entitled to make a fool of himself if he's ready to pay the cost. It cost me 12 years.*

And so, here we are now, staring directly at the fourth wall.

It's called the *Illusion of Choice* and turns inmates into zombies.

This wall is invisible to the prisoner. His untrained eyes cannot see that his behaviors stem from underlying forces of which he is unconscious.

That's why he typically protests that his 'decisions' are entirely of his own making, and always have been.

This wall can be summarized in ten words:

> *You think you know what you're doing but you don't!*

Obedient Zombies

Too many people sleepwalk through life. They think they're making their own choices but they're not.

From childhood on, they stagger through life, mindlessly reacting to their upbringings and environment.

> *They obey and do whatever they're told.*
>
> *Or they engage in <u>negative</u> obedience and mindlessly do the <u>opposite</u> of whatever they're told.*

Either way, life proves desperately unfulfilling, and, all too often, dangerous; Mother Nature doesn't have a bullet with your name on it; she has millions of bullets inscribed "to whom it may concern."

Time Travel to Rikers

Come time travel with me. Cross the two lane so-called Bridge of Pain and arrive on Rikers Island. Pass through the iron gates, stride down the corridors, then step down into the basement cell, masquerading as my classroom.

Here we are then. So, take a back seat, and eavesdrop on an early discussion with Kenny Johnson, the cat-burglar and stick-up man who went on to co-found the Eagles with me, and his best friend, Joe Roberts, whom he met in a half-way house, and whom you'll meet later.

"So, Kenny you wound up here in Rikers," I said, "because you got busted for assault—and you were high at the time, right?"

"Yeah, that's what they got me for. I saw this Vic—that's short for *victim*—a chump who won't fight for his wallet. So I crossed the street . . . and stepped right in front of this little old fogey. Gimmee me your wallet, I said. And you know what? The little weasel tried to negotiate. 'Listen Buddy,' I said, this ain't a dialogue, this's a monologue. I ain't askin' I'm tellin'—and I gotta gun in my pocket . . .' I've pulled this routine before. But this time a doorman saw me hanging out and called the cops. They showed up fast and they really did have guns—which I never did, which was just as well, 'cos I'd be serving a whole lot more time. They cuffed me and shipped me off, and here I am."

Kenny was sure he knew what he was doing, but I saw that story differently, and I share my take in a moment.

A Devil Made Me Do It

At one time or another we all say, "Hey—I don't know what came over me!" Or maybe, "the devil made me do it." And if you ever said that, you're on the right track, because we're seldom truly in charge of our actions.

I wrote about this whole subject—free will—in my book, *Wareham's Way*. Some 30-plus years later, Harvard Professor Sam Harris gave the subject some thought, and came to the same conclusions:

> *The idea that we as conscious beings are deeply responsible simply can't be mapped onto reality. No-one picks their parents, or the society to which they were born. No-one picks the moment in history into which they were born. No-one picks their genes or the environment influences which determine the structure of their brain. You didn't pick your soul, if you have one. Your brain is making choices based upon beliefs and intentions and states that have been hammered into it over a lifetime. So, how can we be free, if everything we consciously intend was caused by things we did not intend and of which we're entirely unaware? We can't.*

I agree, of course:

We're mostly unaware of where our thoughts and goals come from. And we mostly don't have conscious control of them either.

Some moments before you are aware of what you will do next—a time in which you seem to be making a free choice—your brain has already chosen your next action.

You then become conscious of the 'decision' and believe that you are in the process of making it.

BUT

> that's just an illusion—the *Illusion of Choice*;
> <u>you think you know what you're doing but you don't</u>.

Forces we're unaware of create that Zombie in the fourth wall and leave him staggering from one crisis to another.

The Justice Conundrum

For sure, our system of justice should reflect an understanding that fate could have dealt any one of us a different hand of cards.

But belief in free will has delivered two low spades: the religious conception of 'sin' and our commitment to so-called retributive justice.

Yes, of course, some people are so dangerous that they need to be incarcerated.

But if there's no free will, blame and vengeance are unhelpful. Even terrifying sociopaths can seem like victims.

But closed-minded lawmakers dislike honest discussion of criminal behavior because it seems to excuse immoral behavior.

These are not new or new-fangled ideas. Think about the advice shared with prisoners of the Cook County Jail, Chicago, way back in 1902 by Clarence Darrow, a lawyer who defended notorious clients in famous trials:

> *People are not in jail because they deserve to be.*
> *They are there because of circumstances entirely*
> *beyond their control and for which they are in no*
> *way responsible. Most of you do not know why you*
> *committed your crimes—but I do. You did these things*

*because you were bound to do them. It looked to you
at the time as if you had a chance to do them or
not, as you saw fit, but in fact, you had no choice.
There may be people here who had some money in
their pockets and who still went out and got some
more money in a way society forbids. Now you may
not yourselves see exactly why it was you did this
thing, but if you look at the question deeply enough
and carefully enough you would see that there were
circumstances that drove you to do exactly the thing
which you did. You could not help it any more than
we outside can help taking the positions that we take.*

What I would add to that is this:

*If we cannot conceive of a viable option, then for us it
does not exist.*

We never had a choice—just the *Illusion of Choice*. So should
anyone go to jail for that?

If Clarence Darrow or Malcolm X were here right now,
they'd explain that Kenny was a victim of the *Illusion of Choice*.

In the moment of crossing the street to rob his victim,
Kenny could conceive of no other viable option—and so no
other choice existed, not for him anyway.

"Yeah, I get it now," said Kenny after he was
released and then returned with me to Rikers as
a respected Eagles teacher. "I was a zombie back
then, too. So, now, we gotta find a way to get a
lightbulb inside every inmate and at-risk kid."

So, yes, if you wound up in prison, you were indeed a victim,
because, in the moment of committing your so-called crime,
you never had a choice, either—only the illusion of a choice.

If you had a weapon it may have been a threat, a fist, a boot, a knife, or a gun. It may have been the nod of your head, or the down-turning of your thumb. It may even have been silence in the presence of potential violence or death. Whatever the missile, it had been a long time in the making.

Becoming a casualty was outside your control. It was something that happened to you. That is not just an excuse. That is an explanation. That is the truth.

But now, today, right in this moment, armed with new insights, you can make a conscious, rational choice. You can choose never to be a victim again. And you can choose a whole new life.

The Invisible Door

And now you see it! It was invisible before, but now you can see a door in the middle of that fourth wall—the Door of Understanding.

Aha, yes—*enlightenment*. In Japan they call it the moment of *satori*. Taoists say that to be enlightened is to be in harmony with the universe. Christians say it's about being reborn and putting away childish things.

My own take is that it's all about waking up and getting real.

Happily, the great thing about landing in jail, as the philosopher Gurdjieff observed, is that:

> *awakening begins when a man realizes that he is going nowhere and doesn't know where to go.*

With the *Illusion of Choice* in play, you've been seeing the world "as through a glass darkly".

Your personal polaroids were blocking so much light that you got trapped inside a mental prison.

Like Malcolm X, you were living a zombie-like life that you never truly created.

You couldn't make sense of what was truly happening. But now you can. And now we will.

Good News / Bad News

Let me say it again. Virtually everyone who winds up in jail is a victim. And you're no exception. You were indeed a hapless casualty, as the world—your world—shaped you and shipped you off behind the wall.

But you were sleepwalking then—and you're awake now—right?

Oh Happy Day.

And you're listening carefully, too.

I hope so. Because, let me say it loud and clear:

From this moment on, there can be excuses and no going back—you and you alone are now fully responsible for everything you do.

Happily, that apparent burden also presents you with the greatest opportunity of your life. You'll see why in a just a moment.

In our next sessions we'll *defang the snake* who poisoned your outlook, *emasculate the gremlin* who pushed you down dead-end alleys, and *expose the witch* who duped you, doped you, and ditched you.

We'll start with the venomous reptile.

This will involve you in another time-travel trip back to Rikers. You'll join the class, and as they did for me, the guys in green will change the way you think about your life and your world.

A Mysterious Stranger

As you pass out of the darkness and into the light, let's think about the Zen story of the man who meets a sublimely, almost magically confident and poised stranger.

"Are you a god?" says the man.

"No," comes the reply.

"Are you a sorcerer?"

"No."

"Are you a genius?"

"No."

"What are you then?"

"I am awake," says the Buddha.

The Bottom Line

And so, here now, Eagles graduate and my special friend, Richard Moore, shares a profound personal lesson from our little book, *How to Survive a Bullet to the Heart*:

> *Criminal conduct is wrong doing. My doings—my actions—truly were wrong. I was a negative, hurtful influence. I harmed countless people, and I was blind to the harm I caused. Then I woke up.*
>
> *So, what is remorse? Looking backwards and shaking my head in wonderment that I was the benumbed zombie who did all those terrible things wasn't enough. Saying "I'm sorry" was a good start, but not enough, either. Yes, we will look back and shake our heads and say we're sorry. But it means nothing unless we act. A truly remorseful person gives back by helping others. We become productive, law-abiding citizens. We show our children the right doings. We set them onto right roads.*
>
> *Real remorse is real growth, honest to goodness, once*

*and forever change. As we Eagles like to say, the lower
we fall, the higher we can rise.*

Ah yes, there are no mistakes in life, just lessons.

The sleepwalker who wakes doesn't need to change himself.

Instead, what he suddenly realizes is that he has been dreaming. And that he can set his world aright, and create a life he'd like to share with everyone around him.

And so *The Breakout Plan* is dedicated to the memory of George Floyd, the man they called the gentle giant, whose mindless and brutal killing while in the custody of zombies may have awakened in all of us the need to set our worlds aright.

The Wall of the Snake

Before You Know It, Heartache Follows

Yes, yes, of course. We only pay attention to the things that we discover for ourselves. And sometimes the lessons come late.

I was looking for a something to steal from a backwater bookstore when my teenage eyes locked onto the melancholy face of a beautiful dark woman.

Her image graced the cover of a book, *Thursday's Child*. As they looked up from the cover of that autobiography, those sad eyes of hers were surely saying something to me. I grabbed the book and flicked through the pages.

Then I left the store with the lovely little tome under my arm.

Her story intrigued me. And she became known the world over for her come-hither looks and smoky voice. I bought all her records, but that was it. Our paths never crossed.

But then, to my amazement, 50 years later, on the other side of the world, and out of the clear blue yonder, she called me. When we get to the end of this chapter, I'll tell you why, and what we talked about.

But the lesson she taught me is the message I'll be sharing with you right now.

Recap

But first, let's recap our last session. You'll recall, I hope, that all prisons are mental prisons. And every mental prison has 4 walls, a door, a lock, and a key. They lock from the inside and you hold the key—so only you can let yourself out. We call this the 4-Walls Model. You can never get out of prison—or stay out—until you understand how these four walls lock together and trap you inside.

And before you can even see that door or turn that key, you need to know that a snake, a gremlin, a beautiful, merciless lady—a witch, actually—and a zombie are alive within those four walls. And they'll fight like hell to hold those walls in place, and you trapped inside.

In our last session, we woke our zombie—and showed him the fourth wall, the *Illusion of Choice*. Don't forget that wall, the *Illusion of Choice*. You got it, right? It was why you could conceive of no viable option to the actions you took that loused up your life.

But, now that we're awake to that wall, we can reveal the *snake*, the *gremlin*, and the *witch* who live inside the other three walls.

SNAKEBITE

So, now, come time travel with me back to Rikers Island. Pull up a plastic chair in the basement classroom of the second session of the second class I ever ran. And let's check out that venomous snake and slap a label on the wall.

"Instead of a prepared speech," I said to the guys in green, "let's each of you grab some feelings of liberation by sharing"—I turned to the blackboard, grabbed a stub of white chalk, and scrawled, *The Story of My Life*. Well, what I heard that morning changed my life. You'll know why after you hear the words of Eugene, a proud, slim sensitive 20 year-old inmate.

I grew up in Harlem. My father took off when my mother got pregnant. It was just me and my mother, and my grandmother. My mother was sick most of the time. She was on crack. My grandmother was my real mother. She cared for me and I loved her. I really loved her. Then, when I was nine, my mother overdosed and died. So now my grandmother was the only person in my life. We lived and slept in the same rented room. It was a rough neighborhood. Guys wanted anything you had—money, chains, jacket, whatever. If you had nothing to give them you could get beaten up. My grandmother worried I'd get a bashing. That happened more than a couple times, too. So she walked me the five blocks to school. The guys didn't like that. They would follow us, walking way too close, and talking trash and laughing at her and me both. Sometimes they tossed real rubbish, too. My grandmother also tried to meet me on the way home. I was always thrilled and relieved to see her. She always gave me a loving hug. Then one day . . . I saw her in the distance, running towards me. But something was wrong . . . Her hair was orange and she was waving her arms and screaming. Then I saw what'd happened . . . They'd thrown gasoline on her and set her on fire. Her clothes were burning. And so was her hair. She died in hospital that night. And I got sent to an orphanage. You can imagine what happened there. If it wasn't for you guys in this class, I'd be alone in the world.

Depressing, right?

Well, the pain and passion in every one of those life stories was a shocker. What I saw, first hand, right there in that forlorn cell, what became indelibly imprinted into my brain cells, was that emotional damage had been inflicted, and every inmate was a deeply wounded prey. Physical scars had healed but emotional wounds were no longer invisible.

Suffering showed in every word and face. If a journey to redemption has to pass through a confessional box then that's what my class became that day . . . I'd been exposed to something as special as it was dark. I resolved right then and there to change the world by making sense of those stories.

"Okay you guys, we gotta learn something from what you just shared." I reached back into my mind for something to say. Happily, I recalled some favorite lines from a play:

None of us can help the things that life has done to us. They're done before you realize it. And once they're done, they make you do other things. Until at last everything comes between you and what you'd like to be, and you have lost your true self forever.

"Not a happy thought right? BUT, my take is that we can reverse that process by getting a handle on those things that life does to us before we realize it. So before our next class, I'm gonna get you another poem to think about. And, the subject of next week's speech will be 'the person or philosophy that most influenced my life.'"

Manhood?

Something about those life stories stuck in my brain. I researched the guys in that Rikers Class:

13—almost half, did not know their fathers.

7—a quarter said their father was dead.

6—a fifth, said their fathers were addicts.

3—said their father was abusive.

1—had a father who cared but couldn't help.

So, so, so!

> With no father around, how does a man
> learn to be a man?

Back on Rikers next Monday, David's speech to the
class pretty well answered my question:

> *I grew up in the slums. Such beautiful*
> *sounds: sirens, gunshots, people yelling*
> *and cussing, fighting and arguing, bottles*
> *being broken. To me it was all a sweet*
> *serenade, the loveliest lullaby ever sung.*
> *I was drawn to the flashing lights like a*
> *baby to a teat, especially on hot summer*
> *nights, when the crazy shit is happening.*
> *The sun goes down and the lights come*
> *up. Now you see the action. Now you*
> *see the hustlers, the pushers, the pimps,*
> *the junkies, the hoes, the addicts, the con*
> *men. They were all superheroes to me. I*
> *cruised the streets with my friends until*
> *the wee hours. Then came the day my*
> *mother locked me out. 'You never come*
> *home and you love the streets,' she said,*
> *'so now they're yours.'*
> *But this was great! Now I could party*
> *forever. It was cool with me. But then*
> *the seasons shifted. Suddenly everybody's*
> *going to school, shopping, getting all*
> *freshed up. And I'm still wearing the*
> *same clothes I wore all summer.*
> *It's hard to keep up at school when you're*
> *homeless. Homework is hard when you got*
> *no home. How do you show up at school*

when last night you slept on a roof, or in someone's
car? Who do I turn to for help? I turn to the streets.
The streets showed me how to survive. They taught me
how to deal drugs. And to lie and to steal and to rob.
They drugged me and put me on the road to prison.
When I woke up the streets had disappeared. Now
there were only walls. Fuck the streets. You can have
that bitch to yourself. I just want to go home.

So there it was: the triple whammy of the absent father
syndrome: neglect, a rotten environment, the education of
the streets—and, of course, a woeful outcome. Even more
startling to me was that of all but one of the others chose the
same person; 'my mother'. The odd man out was Eugene who
chose his grandmother. Wow!

It was time to make some sense of all this. I
stepped to the front of the class.

"Okay you guys you all read the poem right?"

"It was bamboozling Teach."

"Yes—it can seem confusing. But the message
is deep. Listen up. I'll read it aloud, then we'll see
what we can all make of it. Here we go:

A lash of brightness catches you off guard
in childhood. It completes you.
                    You change size
in dreams of smelly water, catch your eyes
impersonating something bright and hard
as sun and moon wear hot grooves
                    in the sky
and you lurch toward conclusion.
Here your strange illumined limbs
                    betray you.

You must change unrestingly now.
        You, swollen and sly,
must welcome turmoil as a central friend
who plies her fangs of difference
        through your heart.
And now you're anyone's to break apart.
And now you're anyone's
        to bind and bend.
You will not understand, but will endure,
snakebit, and never dreaming of a cure.

"So what's this guy trying to tell us?"

"That things go off the rails," said Leigh.

"So it seems. Let's think about the first line, *A lash of brightness catches you off guard in childhood.*"

"He's sayin' you get a taste of the lash when you're a kid."

"What kind of lash?"

"It changes you," said Luke.

"Right— *You change size / in dreams of smelly water, catch your eyes / impersonating something bright and hard / as sun and moon wear hot grooves in the sky / and you lurch toward conclusion . . .*"

"So what's all this about hot grooves?" said Celso.

"He's sayin' the world seems weird—and that's making you weird too," said Leigh.

"So are you changing for the better or worse?" I asked

"Worse. It's like you got sucker-punched."

"Right, and then, *your strange illumined limbs betray you.'*

"You're punch-drunk and wobbly," said Celso. You must change *unrestingly* now.

"Gotta man-up and protect yourself."

"Right—listen carefully to the next three lines."

You, swollen and sly / must welcome turmoil as a central friend / who plies her fangs of difference through your heart.

"You got gnawed by the viper."

I jumped in. "With *fangs of difference*, right? What might they be?" Long pause. "Might you feel like an outsider? Maybe you even feel like, even, uh, that you're the, uh, wrong . . . color?"

"I ain't the wrong color," said Kenny. "None of us is."

"You sure about that?" said Celso.

"Maybe some of us hide those feelings," said Michael.

"And maybe that's where turmoil comes in," said Leigh.

"Yeah, like an ass-hole buddy you can't shake off," said Kenny.

"Right—that's a great answer. But what do these next two lines mean?

And now you're anyone's to break apart / And now you're anyone's to bind and bend . . ."

"That you're a patsy and a victim and a loser," said Kenny.

"Right again! So what do we make of these final lines?"

You will not understand, but will endure / snakebit, and never dreaming of a cure.

"You'll live but you won't get over being bitten," said Leigh.

"Right—but *never dreaming of a cure.*" I could see that I didn't need to spell that message out.

"Let's read the whole poem again."

"I'll do it," said Kenny.

His smoky rap-rhythm filled the cell.

After the last line, he looked up and smiled, "And that, my brothers, was *Sss-Nake-Bite . . .* by Maximillian Philips."

A soft round of applause followed.

I waited.

"So, what kind of personal snakebites are we talking about? Who else got bitten by the snake?"

"My grandmother . . . they set her on fire," said Gene.

"I cruised the streets," said Hutch. He paused. "Then my mom locked me out of the house."

"Maybe you were snakebit already," I said: "No father, pimps and thieves for heroes, all of that—"

"None of us had fathers," said Thomas. "Not proper dads."

And so it went.

"Let's get it out in the open. One way or another, every last one of you guys suffered abuse and neglect. We agree on that, right?" They nodded ruefully.

"*SSSnakebite!*" said Kenny

So, at home we see the snakebite of physical and sexual abuse—and verbal barbs are poison too.

And there's social snakebite, too: a rotten education. The cruelty of the streets. And ongoing racist slurs.

The venom enters the heart and infects real lives. No wonder those lives went off the rails.

Never happened?

In fact most people never realize the fact or the extent of the damage inflicted by the snake.

> "I never got no snakebite as a kid," said Antoine.
>
> "Never?"
>
> He paused, and scratched his head.
>
> "We all got along and my mother kept a nice house . . . well, now that you got me thinkin' . . . I do remember a couple of times when I came home that some people were bleeding to death on the kitchen floor."
>
> Wow . . .
>
> "And you see no connection from that to the fact that you're here because you murdered two men by pushing them off the top of a building?"

SSSnakebite! Antoine had been desensitized to cruelty, even to death itself.

Not all snakebites are so dramatic.

Yet every puncture delivers a lasting wound.

But, most people survive, right?

So does it really matter all that much if people get bitten by the snake?

Yes, one way or another, if they're still with us, people do survive. But no matter how talented they might be, feelings of unworthiness dog their days, and make them incapable of creating the life they were meant to live.

Stuck inside their mental prisons, instead of tackling and surmounting life's problems, they either give up on life, or get high, or join up with the wrong crowd and fall into a life of crime—or all the above.

But wait—there's more.

The O.J. Syndrome

Many snakebite victims try to ease their feelings of unworthiness by becoming celebrated over-achievers. But no matter how great the success, those feelings do not go away.

In fact, as we'll see, they mostly get worse. So, now, all too often, as in a game of snakes and ladders, the overachiever finds a way to sabotage success, and return to square one. O.J. Simpson is a case in point. Harvey Weinstein, too.

Effectively such recidivists are crucified between two thieves: the need for attention and the guilty need for self-punishment.

Unconsciously they ease their anxiety by penalizing themselves, while at the same time drawing the attention of friends and family to their dilemmas, and begging for help and forgiveness.

You will not understand but will endure
Snakebit and never dreaming of a cure.

Here Comes the Enforcer

So *there's* the snake. And, now, as promised, let's slap a label—a poster, in fact—on that wall; we call it the *Wall of Emotional Damage.*

And that wall is more important than you think, because—listen up now—it *creates the gremlin who lives inside the next wall.*

I'll tell you a little more about that in a moment.

But first this:

> John, you gotta tell the guys about the gremlin who
> enforces the psychic contract. That's a <u>huge</u> idea.

My great friend Hassan said that.

So, the gremlin and the contract he enforces are on the plate for our next chapter.

I'll show how the first wall of emotional damage locks into the second wall of a mind unconsciously guided by a loathsome gremlin who leverages the emotional damage of snakebite and enforces a poisoned loser's contract.

You'll also learn how to emasculate that gremlin, and set yourself up for lifelong freedom.

The Phone Call

But first, as promised, let's get back to that phone call.

"I'm Eartha," she purred. "Eartha Kitt." There was no mistaking that sultry, silky voice. "I'm performing just a few blocks away from you at the Carlyle. A fan gave me a copy of your *Wareham's Way* book just last night. I'm liking it so much I got your phone number, and called to say it's a helpful gem."

"Wow! What page are you onto?"

"I have it right here," she said. "I'm at the top of page 119."

"Well, thanks. I'm flattered." And I truly was. My book was about self-sabotage and how to fix it. The sad eyes on the cover of her book flashed into my mind.

"And, um, you know what, as a kid I was, ah, tempted to steal a copy of your autobiography. The title's still stuck in my mind, *Thursday's Child.*"

"Naughty boy," she laughed. "Did you give in to that temptation?"

"Something in the way your photo looked up from the cover told me not to. So I dug deep and paid full price."

"And you still remember that moment."

"I never forgot the book, either. Your words inspired me."

We chatted about her rags to riches journey from little Eartha Mae to legendary Eartha Kitt.

Then, after I cradled the phone, I stepped to my bookshelf, grabbed my copy of *Wareham's Way*, and turned to page 119.

Ah, yes. Right at the top of the page—an adult life quote from Judy Garland, the former child star of *The Wizard of Oz*.

'If I'm a legend why am I so unhappy?'

Ah, yes: yet another scar. *Sssnakebite*. But let Eartha tell what went down:

> My mother gave me to this family because the man
> she wanted to marry said I don't want this yellow girl
> in my house. So, being an illegitimate child and the
> wrong color, you are not wanted by the whites and
> the blacks couldn't care less. So this black family, who
> had two teenage children, they tied a sack around
> my waist, then tied me to a tree, and with a peach
> tree switch they would beat my bottom until I was
> bleeding and I only had one thing to wear and that
> was also made of potato sacking . . . and she's trying
> so hard to find somebody that says Eartha Mae, it's
> all right, you are wanted, too.

Snakebite—how does one deal with it? Who can a child turn to? The safe strategy, alas, is silence and secrecy—which, of course, merely sends the poison deeper into the heart:

> That little ugly duckling was always told she's an ugly
> duckling. Nobody wants you. While this was going on
> I couldn't tell anybody about it, because who would
> have believed it?

So what to do? Some people say, get over it, and some people say that they have. But snakebite never quite goes away:

> I take off the makeup and I'm not Eartha Kitt any more. I'm Eartha Mae again. It becomes a testing ground. And I know that. No matter how hard you try not to, it's still there.

But, as promised, here's the message for us to take away today:

> I'm very glad that I can have the feelings from that urchin. And I'm very glad that I have never tried to cover her up. I'm very glad that she's still a part of me. And I'm very glad that she will always be a part of me—because she helps me do what I know I have to do.

Yes, like Eartha, we can extract wisdom and empathy from snakebite and use it to create an awareness of the purpose of our human existence.

The Cure

So, let me make it crystal clear:

> The deepest antidote for snakebite begins with seeing and accepting that it is merely one of four walls that lock together to become a mental prison.

By truly understanding that predicament we can begin to see a pathway to a whole new life.

So, here's where we've gotten to:

- First, you now realize that you were sleepwalking through life until you saw the *Wall of the Illusion of Choice.*

- And, now we've identified the *Wall of Emotional Damage—sssnakebite*; we've seen how it creates anxiety and turmoil in our lives.

So, now we begin to see how to transform snakebite from a curse to a blessing.

In our next session we'll see how the gremlin tries to put a stop to that, by leveraging the *Wall of Emotional Damage* into the unhappiest of outcomes.

For now, it'll surely help to remember that:

> *Life is too brief,*
> *between the budding and the falling leaf,*
> *to lose our lives in long-gone grief,*
> *or shape a fate with wounding words.*
> *In kindness and in gentleness our speech*
> *must carry messages of hope and reach*
> *the sweetest chords.*

The Wall of the Gremlin

The 24/7 Enforcer In Your Brain

It doesn't matter if the Breakout Plan is reaching you in a prison cell.

What *does* matter, is to understand why good people wind up in prison.

In our nifty little book of inmate poetry, *How to Survive a Bullet to the Heart*, my good friend Sheldon shares the opening move in his journey:

> I'd worked all summer and I'd just gotten paid. I bought a new pair of sneakers and a new leather jacket. I couldn't wait to get back to school to show it all off. But on my way home a street gang demanded I give them my sneakers and jacket.

So, what to do in such a situation? Deliver the goods, or turn tail and run? We'll see what Sheldon did in just a moment.

But first, let's recap our last session.

- As you know, all prisons are mental prisons. And every mental prison has four walls, a door, a lock, and a key. They lock from the inside and you hold the key—so only you can let yourself out. We call this the 4-Walls Model. You can never get out of prison—or stay out—until you understand how these four walls lock together and trap you inside.

- And before you can even see that door or turn that key, you need to know that a zombie, a snake, a gremlin, and a beautiful, merciless lady—a witch, actually—are alive within those four walls. And they'll fight like hell to hold those walls in place, and you trapped inside.

- In our first session, we woke our zombie—and showed him the fourth wall, that being, the *Illusion of Choice*. It was why you could conceive of no viable option to the actions you took that loused up your life.

- In our second session we defanged the snake in the *Wall of Emotional Damage*—the source of anxiety and turmoil that turns your dreams into nightmares. We'll meet the beautiful, merciless *witch* next session.

The gremlin

Right, now, let's shine a light on the gremlin.

He's *your* gremlin and he wants two things.

- First, he's a fake friend who wants to push a bunch of opinions that make you feel lousy.

- Second, as we'll see, he also wants to enforce what we call a loser's psychic contract.

On that subject, here's a message from Hassan:

> *Fellas, this is Hassan again, and I'm jumping in to say that in my humble opinion this session right now blends two especially big ideas: the loser's poisoned psychic contract and the gremlin inside our brains who enforces it. These concepts are deeper and sharper than anything I ever heard in any prison program—and, needless to say, I've heard and participated in dozens of them. So, sit back, and, in the spirit of brotherhood, listen up like your life depends upon it. Peace.*

Okay then. I'm betting that you already have some sense of your gremlin.

- He's a creation of your snakebites.
- He's always with you, waking and sleeping.

- He defines and interprets your every experience.
- He's a bully whisperer who makes you relive past mistakes, worry about the future, and joylessly pick apart the people in your life.

And he pursues these loathsome goals with subtlety and cunning. But, as we'll see in a moment:

The deadliest thing about your gremlin, is that, until you wake to his presence in your brain, he often comes disguised as the voice of intuition.

BELIEFS AND WHISPERS

First, though, let's think about those opinions the gremlin wants to push, because they're the bricks in your *Wall of Imprisoning Beliefs.*

Here's the thing: *A belief is an opinion not a fact.*

We mostly pick up these opinions without noticing where they came from.

And we're mostly unaware of what we actually believe.

But—and stay with me now, because this is a big idea—even when our beliefs are just plain wrong, we cherish what we believe is a sacred right to hold onto 'our' beliefs.

We do that because we think our so-called principles make us free.

BUT, in fact, our beliefs—which all too often are the gremlin's cunning whispers—merely force us to live our lives in accordance with illusions—and thereby imprison us.

To survive a rotten upbringing, a snakebit child typically learns to believe that:

- *people around me can't be trusted to look after me;*
- *so, I need to yell to get what I need;*

- *and, if I'm hungry, it's okay to steal;*
- *and I'm not learning anything, so I might as well skip school.*

Such beliefs may be true at the time. For sure they help that child to survive childhood, and grown-ups may laughingly call that kid a scallywag.

BUT

when these beliefs get carried over into adult life, they result in trouble—maybe even a stint in prison.

That Gremlin's Whispers

Let's get back to Sheldon's leather jacket and sneakers, and see how Sheldon's gremlin set about destroying him. Here's what Sheldon said:

> *I wasn't going to part too easily with what I'd earned. Words escalated into a fight. The gang leader drew a knife and stabbed me and I got rushed to the hospital. Until then, I believed I was safe in my community—or at least untouchable. But now I realized that evil is real, and that the world was made up of predators and prey. I thought that to survive I needed to pick a side. I made a promise to protect myself and my family from predators, so I bought my first gun. But as time passed I realized I wasn't playing defense anymore. Now I was on offense. I'd become what I despised, a predator. I tried to tell myself that I was only robbing hustlers and drug dealers. But robbing led to more of the same, and all too soon I wound up in Central Bookings.*

So, as you can see, when we take a close look at Sheldon's words, we can also hear the mental gremlin gulling Sheldon into accepting a bunch of imprisoning beliefs:

I believed I was untouchable . . .
> No worries, you're safe.

I wasn't going to part too easily with what I'd earned.
> It'll be okay to risk your life for your jacket.

I needed to pick a side.
> Becoming a hoodlum is your wisest choice.

I made a promise to protect myself and my family from predators.
> Yeah, family comes first, so get yourself a gun.

I was only robbing hustlers and drug dealers.
> Get what you want, 'cos these low-lifes don't matter.

Sad, right?

As you see, our *thoughts* spring from our *feelings*—then generate a *belief* that causes an *action*.

Then, as the calm reasoning side of the brain figures out a solution, the gremlin slips unnoticed into our thinking and raises all kinds of doubts and fears:

> *Who do you think you are?*
> *You're just a loser. You're gonna fail again if you try to do the right thing.*
> *Quit now before you make even more of a fool of yourself.*

And so, instead of following the wisdom of our own hearts and minds, we give up on our dreams and stay stuck in our mental prisons, feeling lousy.

Something to think about, right?

But put that onto the back burner for now. Let's share an imaginary journey and answer four questions along the way.

The Mountain and the Stone

1.   You have set off to climb a mountain in search of a fabulously rare stone. *What is your impression as you stand at the foot of the mountain and look up at it?*

2.   After a hard search, you haven't found the stone, and now the sun has fallen. *What will you do next?*

3.   You have finally discovered the stone you were seeking. *What kind of stone is it? Describe its size, weight, and value.*

4.   Now it is time to come down from the mountain and return home. *What parting words do you have for the mountain, and what is its reply?*

While you're thinking about your answers, let me say that this mountain you just climbed is an introduction to what I call a *Psychic Contract.*

> *This is the huge idea that Hassan says could rescue just about every inmate and everyone at risk of winding up inside such a prison cell.*

- So, for openers, that mountain symbolizes the father you looked up to as a kid.

- And the journey is all about overcoming that daunting presence, and discovering the precious jewel of your own true self.

- If the challenge seems too great, or the value of the stone too low, you've still got work to do.

- Pay close attention to the parting words.

- Put-downs may signal what I call a *poisoned* psychic contract, which we'll get to in just a moment.

It'll also be helpful to think about the challenges of your parents, and how *their* successes or failures are playing out in *your* life. But right now, think about this . . .

THE PSYCHIC CONTRACT

W hat I've seen with my own eyes, as maybe you have, too, is that the children of corrections officers become corrections officers.

And the children of inmates become inmates.

And, all too typically, *the children from the same family of corrections officers wind up supervising the children from the same family of inmates.*

Why is that?

Before we answer, it may help to know that I earned a lifetime income spotting and developing leaders—or, as some say, sorting winners from losers. Among the things I discovered was that the gremlin does more than tell us what to believe.

He also enforces a Poisoned Loser's Psychic Contract.

This truly is a big idea, so stay with me now.

The Contract

It all begins when, unaware of what they're doing, after observing the lifestyle in their homes, most children strike a *Psychic Contract* in their heads and hearts that defines success in life as equaling or marginally outperforming their parents in terms of status or income.

Just as we're unaware of creating that contract, we're also mostly unaware that we're devoting our daily lives to fulfilling it.

In adult life this psychic contract eventually morphs into a *culminating event*—a milestone at a turning point—that signals completion of the contract.

Trouble is, many parents don't want their kids to outdo them. So they poison the contract with a kicker: whatever you do you're gonna fail or wind up in jail.

So, the culminating event might just as well be to fail in a business as to start one.

Or, having become a schoolteacher, to get fired.

Or, instead of making a clean getaway, to get caught red-handed while attempting rob a bank.

You might think I'm joking, but I'm afraid not.

Absent Father?

And what about the absent parent syndrome? By default, kids without parents mostly assume the status of the missing father. And the psychic contract is just to survive. And of course, street kids mostly follow heroes who survive the streets and acquire ritzy clothes, cars, and women—as my great friend Big Bear, notes:

> *Being poor and black from the hood, I thought it*
> *was natural for me to do the things that I was doing.*
> *I thought it was socially acceptable for me to hang*
> *out all day and night getting into mischief, drinking,*
> *selling drugs, trafficking guns—I pretty much did it all.*

Other Real-Life Gremlins

As mentioned earlier, my class completed a series of sentences, one of which was, *I'm in jail because . . .*

We can surely hear the gremlin's voice in these all-too-typical responses

Mel: *I'm in jail because* <u>I am an idiot.</u>

Adam: *I'm in jail because* <u>of my dumb ways of thinking.</u>

Nobody who ever gave himself such a put down, quit the program. They stayed the course, read the material, and joined the discussions.

Every one of them was insightful and smart.

None of them was dumb or stupid.

None was an idiot or a fool.

Many of the inmate poems we gathered were similarly revealing.

> *I dreamed that night of Gail, she of the sultry smile*
> *and tail,*
> *and of how now /she'd likely drop a veil*
> > *for some local stud*
> > *by the name of Dale.*
> > <u>You better get depressed 'cos your girl's gone off</u>
> > <u>with toffy nosed winner.</u>

Or this one . . . .

> *I was tired of being broke and bummy.*
> *I wanted some real cash in a hurry*
> *And I gotta get it, by any means necessary.*
> > <u>Yeah get it any way you can</u>
>
> *If it doesn't make dollars, it doesn't make sense to me.*
> > <u>Yeah—Gotta get Big money</u>

As you see, it all makes perfect sense to the gremlin enforcing the psychic contract.

An Unexpected Lesson

Let's get back to Rikers. I was sharing some thoughts with the guys in green about their responses of the class to an incomplete sentence on choosing a career.

"You gotta read em what I wrote," said Wilfredo.

He was barely out of his teens, short, not so good looking, and sitting in the front row.

I scanned the page and found his response to the open-ended sentence, *If I could have any career* . . . As I glanced at him he smirked. A smirk can hide a lot of pain.

"You're sure you want me to read this out loud for everyone?"

'Yeah, you *gotta* read it," he said.

"Okay then, if you say so. You wrote, '*If I could have any career I'd be a porno star because I like having sex with females for money.*'"

Wilfredo glanced back over his shoulder, doubtless looking for approval. But the laughter was muted. And the senior guys looked to me.

"Well, it's kind of funny, right, Wilfredo?" He nodded. "And it's also very insightful, so thanks for that."

"You gonna give us, your take John?" said a voice in back.

I glanced to Alfredo. "You're happy for us to discuss this, right?"

"Yeah, yeah, yeah. Give it your best, Teach," he said.

"Well, my understanding is that becoming a real-life porn star is easier for a gal than a guy. The money they pay a guy is chickenfeed. And for that, he has to maintain an erection—naked and under lights with people running around—and often for hours every day." Alfredo looked a little worried. "And suicide is pretty common in the porn profession. So we might want to think about all that . . . But, on a deeper level . . ."

"Yeah, go deeper, John," said the voice in back.

"My take, Alfredo, is that . . . you might be confusing sex with love. My take is that you might be looking for the love you never got . . .

My take is that you might just want to get even with your mother by compelling her to lie back like an animal and give you what you want"—he began to raise a fist—"while you get even with her by demeaning the very place you sprang from. And my take is that a gremlin inside your brain has been telling you to do just that, and then put yourself down by bragging about it. And my take, Alfredo, is that you're a smart guy and that the deepest part of you already knows all of that"—he dropped the fist—"so, really, thanks for sharing this insight here today. You've shown all of us a lesson that we can move on from."

The smirk became an accepting smile. And the voice from the back caught the sense of relief in the room.

"Yeah, we got it, John—we *all* did."

Winners and Losers

Okay, let's talk about winners and losers.

- <u>Positive</u> culminating events, like perhaps creating a successful rap group, confer the right to be regarded as a winner.

- <u>Negative</u> culminating events, such as incarceration, typically confer the label of loser.

Remember the Eagle (on page 2) who thought he was a chicken? That very thought was an imprisoning belief. So the Eagle was a big time loser. His culminating event, seeing another Eagle in the sky, came way too late for him revise his psychic contract.

But are you always a loser if you wind up in jail?

That depends upon whether you succeed or fail to fulfill a contract that *only ever exists inside your head.*

A big drug deal might make you a winner but getting busted would make you a loser.

But what if you thought it was okay to get busted? That's a good move, sometimes, right?

You can be a legit winner in anything you do, just so long as *you're* happy with *your* culminating event. But, and listen closely now:

> *if you think that winding up in prison was the move of a loser, then <u>for as long as you hold that belief</u>, you <u>are</u> a loser.*

BUT

> *happily, as we'll soon see, you can reframe that thought in the twinkling of an eye.*

Words

One way to sort winners from losers is to listen closely to what people say:

- *Losers* talk about what they'll do if they win, but they don't know what they'll do if they lose. They mindlessly repeat their errors and look for scapegoats.

- *Winners* have a 'Plan A' for winning BUT they also have secret 'Plan B' that they don't talk about for what they'll do if Plan A doesn't pan out; they acknowledge their mistakes, then consciously eliminate them.

Eagles co-founder Kenny Johnson was so taken by the idea of the psychic contract that he captured the core idea in this poem:

> *I'm one from the flock,*
> *a chip off the old block,*
> *which all adds up to*
> > *I'm just like you, Dad.*

When you were doing well
        you stayed away from us;
When you were doing bad,
        here you cometh
with your mental and physical abuse
saying things like,
        I'll never add up to nothin',
        that I'm of no Goddammed use.
When you look at me
it's like you're staring in the mirror;
manifestation—things are so much clearer:
you hate yourself, and that's a clue
        why you can't love me—because
        I'm just like you, Dad.
Then came the day you gave me
        my first gun.
"Protection" for your only son, was what you said;
        well, image fixed
        and damage done.
I started dissing everyone
I waved that gun and people
        broke into a cockeyed run,
        or froze, and trembled
        in their finest clothes.
And then, one day, to prove
        I was a man, like you,
        I shot—
Well, when those bullets spat
I fast became the coolest cat.
The police my jazz could never quell,
I led them on a hop through hell,
until the night they trapped me
        in a dark motel,

> trashed me with a fond farewell,
> then tossed my bruised and broken body
>> to the steel hotel
>> where I awoke
>> to find myself
>> beside you
>> in the flanking cell.
> So, Mama's words proved all too sad,
> You're like your dad, was what she said.
> Yeah, she foresaw the switcheroo,
> and wept, predicting what she knew;
>> —I'd surely end up
>>> just like you, Dad.

Wow—what a poem. Sums up everything, right?

An inner gremlin pushes imprisoning beliefs that lock us into mental penitentiaries.

He enforces the worst terms of our psychic contracts and delights in making sure we wind up losers.

Beyond the Gremlin

Let's look a little further. You already know that all prisons are mental prisons with a *zombie*, a *snake*, a *gremlin* and a *witch* inside four walls.

We'll defrock the witch in our next session. So far we've identified the zombie inside the *Wall of the Illusion of Choice*, and the snake in the *Wall of Emotional Damage*.

And, in this session, we examined the *Wall of Imprisoning Beliefs* and shared two key ideas:

* First, your gremlin aggravates snakebite wounds, and enforces imprisoning beliefs that trap us in mental prisons and poisoned psychic contracts.

- Second, he's cunning and creative and can whisper unnoticed as a best friend or with the put-downs of a tormenting tyrant.

But you are *not* your gremlin.

You are merely his *observer*—and he has no real hold on you.

And, you feel better—and life gets better—when you start noticing him, and wising up to his true intentions.

THE CURE

So, now, as promised, here's how emasculate that nasty little fellow.

Do it nicely.

When he butts into your brain, acknowledge him politely.

Then, calmly and quietly respond to his poison with the voice of reason.

So let's jump into that exchange.

Here's the gremlin first:

You just screwed up again, you idiot.

> *Hey, there you are Mister Gremlin! Haven't been hearing from you lately. Seems I might have followed some of your silly whispers and slipped up. But there are no mistakes in life, just learning opportunities. And, happily, and as you well know, I'm not now and never have been an idiot. But goodbye now, and thanks for dropping by.*

The gremlin's no idiot, either. He'll see that you've woken to his game, and creep off with his tail between his legs.

But be warned: his visits will taper off, *but* he'll continue scheming for ways to bring you down. So when you least expect it, he'll pop back again.

Now, however, whenever that happens, you'll calmly send him on his way, right?

Here Comes the Witch

In our next session we'll expose the witch—who comes in the form of a beautiful, merciless lady who seduces us and leaves us for dead on the side of the road. We'll discover how to spot and break the spell she casts, and send her back to the hell she came from.

Okay, here's a poem to close this session.

> *The gremlin came a-knocking at my door*
> > *and called my name.*
>
> *I cracked the frame,*
> > *and whispered,*
> > *jaw to jaw:*
>
> *Well, hello my little goblin; sure,*
> > *I hear you kindly*
> > *laying down the law;*
> *but I just aint buying*
> > *what your selling,*
> > *any more.*

There it is . . .

The Wall of the Witch

She Has You Jumping, Then She's Gone

In case you've forgotten, all prisons—including the ones that seem to be made of concrete and steel—are mental prisons.

And they have four interlocking walls—and a door, and a lock, and a key. You hold the key, so only you can let yourself out.

Right now, since you've arrived in this final session on the four walls, I'm betting you really are serious about turning that key, passing through that *Door of Understanding*—and creating a life for yourself outside prison even if right now you still seem to be inside one.

Well, we're just about ready to do that.

So let's kick this session into gear with a question: What do you think might be the common element in these real-life quotes from real inmates?

> Jerome: *When I get outta this Rikers hellhole tomorrow I'm gonna head to the closest watering hole and get smashed.*
> Peter: *She had a kitchen knife right there, and I grabbed it, and I killed her.*
> Sheldon: *Robbing led to killing and the more I did of that, the easier it became . . . I'd become what I despised, a predator.*

Well, what's common to these stories is almost certainly not so simple as you might think. And we'll get to that in just a moment.

A Sassy Poem

First, I'm hoping you'll forgive me for sharing a sassy poem
by my friend, Anthony 'Lucky' Hopkins:

> *Wondering why*
> > *there was so much shit around me*
>
> *I made my first,*
> > *and most profound discovery*
>
> *My head, alas, was stuck up my ass.*
>
> *When sharing*
> > *this startling epiphany*
>
> *I made my second*
> > *most profound discovery:*
>
> *Nobody could hear me.*

Kind of funny, right?

But also a great reinforcement of our 4-Walls model,
comprising:

- *The Wall of the Illusion of Choice*, which creates a
zombie-like blindness to what has been happening in
our lives.

- A *Wall of Emotional Damage* houses a venomous
snake that sinks its fangs into our childhood hearts,
creating anxiety, turmoil and feelings of inferiority.

- *The Wall of Imprisoning Beliefs* now locks into
place. The childhood mind treats the snakebite with
a negative belief system—the core idea being, *I can't get
what I need and want from life unless I cheat*—a viewpoint,
which, in adult life, an inner gremlin exploits to
enforce a poisoned, loser's psychic contract.

So now, we've come to the final wall—and an awaiting
merciless witch who appears in the form of beautiful lady.

A Caveat

You'll recall that when we started on this journey I promised an elegant—but not simplistic—solution to a deceptively simple question:

> Why, when they should know better, do people keep on winding up in unhappy situations?

I'm told that fools can ask questions that wise men cannot answer, and that we only pay attention to the things that we discover for ourselves.

That's why *The Breakout Plan* is a journey of discovery.

And why we use great poems as milestones.

Those verses contain deep and deeply hidden meanings.

Figuring them out is like mining for gold.

Let's see how that works as we time travel to the Rikers basement classroom, where I first introduced the merciless witch to the guys in green.

Stay with me now, as we share some verses from the past that truly do change lives.

THE WITCH

I'd given everyone a copy of a poem that I thought might highlight ingrained self-defeating behaviors. The poet, John Keats, died of tuberculosis back in 1821, at age 25. But his lines hit a deep nerve, and the poem now rates among the hottest 100 all-time poems.

The message proved as powerful as it was subtle. Everyone in the class had met this merciless witch. And, she became part of our shared vocabulary. But I'm getting ahead of myself. Come join the class.

"So you all read the poem, right?" I asked.

"Yeah, but it's kinda fussy old English stuff, so you gotta read it again now," said Kenny. "Cos I'm thinkin' that lady was a witch."

"The actual title, *La Belle Dame sans Merci*, is French for 'The Beautiful Lady Without Mercy.' It's about a traveler who meets a lost knight-at-arms—who looks like a dying deadbeat—on the side of a wintry hill and asks a question. Listen up, cos here we go:

> *O what can ail thee, Knight at arms,*
> *Alone and palely loitering?*
> *The sedge has withered from the Lake*
> *And no birds sing.*

Winter's arrived, my friend, and you look like a sick puppy with no place to go.

> *I see a lily on thy brow*
> *With anguish moist and fever dew,*
> *And on thy cheeks a fading rose*
> *Fast withereth too.*
> *Oh what can ail thee knight at arms*
> *Alone and palely loitering.*

Okay, that was the question. Listen closely now. The first part of the reply, to put it plainly, is that 'I met a great looking babe, and we went back to her place, and, uh, made love.'

> *I met a lady in the Meads,*
> *Full beautiful, a faery's child;*
> *Her hair was long, her foot was light*
> *And her eyes were wild.*
> *She found me roots of relish sweet,*
> *And honey wild, and manna dew,*

And sure in language strange she said—
'I love thee true.'

Okay, you guys, remember *that* line—*in language
strange she said I love thee true*.

She took me to her Elfin grot
And there she wept and sighed full sore,
And there I shut her wild, wild eyes
          With kisses four.
And there she lullèd me to sleep,
And there I dreamed—Ah woe betide!
The latest dream I ever dreamt
          On the cold hill side.

Then I had my *last* dream, and it was a terrible
nightmare.

I saw pale kings, and princes too,
Pale warriors, death-pale were they all;
They cried, 'La Belle Dame Sans Merci
Hath thee hath in thrall.'
I saw their starvèd lips in the gloam,
With horrid warning gapèd wide
And I awoke, and found me here
On the cold hill's side.

And she was gone and he was dying;

And this is why I sojourn here
Alone and palely loitering;
Though the sedge is withered
          from the lake
And no birds sing."

"So what's the moral, Teach?"

"Poems can drill down deep. So here's a
question for you guys: Who was the beautiful lady?"

"Just about any woman I ever met," said Cliff.

"Why don't I doubt that?" said Kenny.

"Come on, tell us. Who was it, Teach?"

"When that beautiful lady spoke in *language strange* she was saying the *opposite* of *I love thee true*. She was saying, 'I have you exactly where I want you, you sonofabitch, and I'm going to destroy you.' And all those kings, princes, and pale warriors, they were all the men who ever wound up in her bed."

"Drugs!" said Kenny. "The beautiful lady is *drugs*—drugs, alcohol, crack, all of that. She said she loved him, and he sure loved her. But she was *killin'* him and he didn't know it. And that's why he wound cold as hell on the side of the road—"

I jumped in—"*where the sedge is withered from the lake and no birds sing*—"

"She doped him, duped him and ditched him," said Kenny.

I turned to the window and felt the sun on my face. "So where might the beautiful lady leave us?"

I gazed through the window bars to the rubble beyond the barbed wire, and then to yellow patchwork of forlorn dandelions struggling to survive within cracks in the tarmac bus route beyond a second barbed wire wall. When I turned back my shadow was on the disinfected linoleum and sunlight had climbed to the knees of those in the front row.

Were they getting it? Would they see for themselves that the beautiful lady had doped them, duped them, and dumped them onto the pock-marked, green plastic chairs within this steel-doored, battered, yellow cell?

"Yeah, we agree on that, Kenny. She doped him and duped him and ditched him. My take is that the beautiful lady is a desire so deep that it becomes an obsession—a passion that seduces us and blinds us and becomes an ingrained habit, a blunder, a routine, a shtick—*a self-defeating behavior*—that torpedoes happiness and leaves us in despair. The very first thing that shtick does is solve the immediate problem. You take a hit, and the world goes away and you feel great—"

"But not for long," said Kenny.

"Right—reality soon comes racing back. And now you're worse off than before. First, because you just reinforced your nasty habit. Second, because now you're hung over—maybe you're even handcuffed. For sure you're sadder than raindrops on a grave."

"And your beautiful lady's gone," said Cliff.

"Yeah, she's gone. So now comes the sting: *instead of accepting responsibility, we sullenly try to shift the blame.*"

"But, nobody's buying *that* story," said Kenny.

So, that was my class. Like I said, the beautiful lady slipped into our discussions. She also generated some great contributions for our book of poems—which is available on Amazon, by the way—under the title *How to Survive a Bullet to the Heart.*

John Wareham

Merciless Beautiful Ladies

British born Neville survived the snakebite of sexual abuse from the chief of the orphanage he wound up in at age eight. Neville tapped his gifts, became a top club manager and concert promoter, moved from London to New York, and ran events for the likes of the Rolling Stones. Alas, his beautiful lady was alcohol. She ditched him, in his early 30's, on the cold hillside of Downstate prison serving a 17 year sentence for vehicular homicide. Here's his take on his beautiful lady.

> When I was young and debonair,
> I courted her, she seemed so fair;
> beguiling eyes and golden hair,
> and teasing lips—and do I dare?
> Alas, I tossed aside all care
> and sought to tame this flying mare;
> imbibing every potion fair
> we trysted in her lover's lair
> —until without a backward glance or care
> she vanished—and to my despair
> I woke to suck on prison air
> within a cell without a prayer.

The merciless witch is no respecter of race, color, creed or class, as Pete's talk to the Downstate class makes doubly clear:

> When I got home that day, my wife was sitting on
> the lounge room floor, boiling up a fix and our newly
> laid carpet was burning, and acid was eating into it.
> It was too much. She had a kitchen knife right there,
> and I grabbed it, and I killed her. It would be easy—all
> too easy—for me to blame my wife. But no, she was
> never that. What I see now is that the beautiful lady

without mercy in my life was my obsession to show
the world that I was a great success. I loved it when I
graduated Harvard with an MBA. I loved that I was
drawing a top salary for managing a top branch of a
top bank. I loved our big house and our BMW. But
when I came home, and saw her doing that again, my
obsession boiled up faster than that acid. And when I
woke, I was here serving a life sentence.

The bitter so-called love story of Andre and his beautiful lady is equally riveting and revealing:

When I was sixteen I was introduced to a beautiful
lady by family and friends. She was well acquainted
with everyone I loved and trusted, so it was easy for
me to embrace her. The more intimate we became, the
more I knew she wasn't no good for me. As they say,
if you love something too much it could be no good
for you. But I loved her to the point that whenever
she was around I would act out, disrespecting my
family and friends, harassing and fighting people—
and breaking the law, often, just to always have her
around. I cannot lie though: she always made me feel
good when we was together, so I thought. But when
she wasn't around and I came back to reality, I was
able to see the effect of her being around me.

Ah yes, Andre got wise to the problem and saw exactly what he had to do:

One day I sat down and told her we couldn't be
intimate no more. I gave her two reasons for splitting:
one, I'm a father now and my daughter's gonna need
my attention more than anything; and, two, every
time I'm around you everything in my life goes wrong.
She understood, or so I thought.

But the wiles and the promises of the beautiful lady are not to be underestimated:

> We went our own ways for a while. But when an obstacle got in my way I would go for a walk to clear my head, and there she would be, waiting with soothing words, and wanting to befriend me. Some nights I would take another path to stay out of her way. One night a friend of mine called my home and invited me to dinner at his house. As I entered his door, there she was sitting at the table, beautiful as ever. Over dinner our eyes locked and we began to talk.

Don't go there, Andre—walk right back out that door, now.

> Then she kissed me and I kissed her back. We got passionate, ignored everyone else, and became intimate that night. Then a fight broke out with my friend and I got involved. When I woke up next morning . . .

Maybe you can guess what happened next? Or maybe not . . .

> When I woke up next morning I was lying in a jail cell trying to remember what happened the night before. 'What am I doing here?' I asked the officer outside my door.
> 'You murdered someone last night,' he said, deadpan.
> 'What happened to the lady that was with me?'
> 'She left with a couple of other guys when she knew you was going to jail for the rest of your life.'
> 'She just left me here?'
> 'We asked her if she was your wife or girlfriend, but she just laughed in our faces. 'No, I don't even remember his name,' she said. 'I just met him tonight.'

Not all self-defeating behaviors result in such tragedies, of course, yet every last one of them creates a needless problem and torpedoes the prospect of contentment.

So let's think back to Jerome—the guy who, upon release from Rikers, went straight to a bar and got drunk. Well, no surprise there, of course, but he landed back inside Rikers less than a month later.

So did he have an alcohol problem?

Not really. Overwhelmed by the challenges ahead, he applied his reliable alcohol *solution*—the perfect example of a self-defeating behavior; it solved his immediate problem, ingrained his habit, and left him worse off than before, looking for someone to blame.

The Moral

So what's the moral then?

Tua, a 20 year-old in my Kiwi class asked a question I'll never forget. "So, John," he said. "Do we think the lady without mercy might somehow be the antidote for snakebite?"

That was a great insight.

Because any kind of self-defeating behavior is an attempt to deal with a deeper issue.

But it is the *wrong* attempt.

What we need to do instead, is find out why we keep on getting into bed with a witch.

So, does that mean that we must give up on our obsessive desires?

Buddhists say yes, but I say not always.

But I also say that what we *must* do is spot the triggers that consistently result in unhappy outcomes. Then figure out why it seems so important to step into that beautiful lady's lair.

John Wareham

In Case You're Lost

Okay then, here's where we've got to. We've seen that every prison has four walls:

- *The Wall of the Illusion of Choice*—the zombie-like blindness of a sleepwalker.

- *The Wall of Emotional Damage*—snakebite suffered that created a set of beliefs that gets us through childhood BUT which locks into—

- The *Wall, of Imprisoning Beliefs,* which comes with an nasty inner gremlin who reinforces negative opinions and beliefs and enforces a loser's psychic contract, which now locks us into—

- *The Wall of Self-Defeating Behaviors,* driven by a witch who seduces us and leaves us for dead.

For anyone you know who has yet to figure out why there might be so much of that aforementioned faeces around him, let me put it all into one sentence:

> *Driven by emotional damage, imprisoning beliefs, and self-defeating behaviors, the unenlightened victim is compelled to act out the self-defeating behaviors that keep him trapped inside the belly of the beast.*

Happily, no matter whether you're behind the wall or not, you now really do know why you landed in a mental prison. So, now that you've passed through the Door of Understanding, our next sessions will guide you as you step into the sunshine and take in the view. To be specific, we'll reveal three tricks—three very big ideas, actually—to healing your heart, making smart choices, and keeping you in top gear as you go zipping along the pathway to creating life that you know in your heart you deserve.

Prison

I'm figuring, this might be a great time to share a poem by my late great friend and Eagles co-founder Kenny Johnson, delivered in his own voice on Eagles graduation day in the Rikers Cell where we ran our classes:

> I made a friend today
> > because I listened
> to every word my brother had to say.
> First, he looks me up and down,
> balls his face into the meanest of a frown
> And spits upon the ground:
> 'You strut like you think you know
> > where it's at.
> But you're a bum to be used
> > as a cheap floor mat,
>
> and I'm just one second
> > from laying you flat.'
> I turn his words within my mind.
> They raise to my eyes a peaceful shine.
> Thank God I left that part of me
> > so very far behind.
> He gets it all right off his chest
> and strides away
> > —then wanders back
> I catch his gaze,
> he shakes my hand:
> > 'Forgive me brother, if you can
> > It's more than threats
> > > that make a man.'
> I made a friend today
> because I listened to every word
> > my brother had to say.

Ah, Kenny—he lit up the skies for so many young guys.

Three Rings around the Sun

What They Spell Is Freedom

So, let me ask a question that changed the world. I kid you not.

I'd arrived early and was alone in the Rikers classroom looking forward to the guys arriving. Kenny came first, treading softly.

"I'm getting out in a month," he said. "And I got an offer of a leadership job. And I'm wondering if you think I should take it."

I was flattered. "What kind of job, exactly?"

"I'd be leading a small team . . . we'd be, uh, robbing a bank."

Yikes. What to say? For sure, a man of Kenny's experience, intellect, and presence would inspire any gangster team.

"Ah, well—what other choices might you have?"

He shot me half a grin. "I got no other offers, but, uh . . . maybe, I could, uh, serve hamburgers at McDonald's. Whattaya think?"

"Well, ah"—guys were entering the room—"let me share my take after the class."

And I did.

And my reply to Kenny changed both our lives, and had a ripple effect that has never stopped.

I'll tell you what I said in a moment. First let's do a lightning recap.

We've seen that every prison has four walls, a door and a lock and a key. You lock yourself in and you hold the key, so only you can let yourself out. The four walls are:

- *The Wall of the Illusion of Choice*—the zombie-like blindness of a sleepwalker;

- *The Wall of Emotional Damage*—snakebite suffered that created a set of beliefs that gets us through childhood BUT which locks into—

- *The Wall of Imprisoning Beliefs*, which comes with a nasty inner gremlin who reinforces negative opinions and beliefs and enforces a loser's psychic contract, which now locks us into—

- *The Wall of Self-Defeating Behaviors*, driven by a witch who seduces us and leaves us for dead.

Happily, no matter whether you're behind the wall or not, you now really do know why you landed in a mental prison. You've turned the key in the Door of Understanding. You're about to embark on a life of freedom. So, in just a moment, we'll look at exactly what you're facing on the morning you step out of prison.

Answering Kenny

Right now, let me share my answer to Kenny, then come join me for some life-changing lessons at Rikers.

"So, Kenny, I figure I'm not qualified to advise you on your choice between robbing a bank and working at McDonalds. So let's have the class debate the subject."

"Howzat work?"

"We'll have two three-man teams—one for and one against. Each of the six speakers will have five minutes to advance his team's argument for or against the motion, *That it is better to rob a bank than work for McDonalds.*

"I'll be on the team that wants to rob the bank?"

"No. You'll learn a whole lot more by leading the team arguing that it's better to work at McDonalds. And we'll have a judging panel, and anyone who wants to share his opinion can be a speaker from the floor."

"Sounds like a courtroom."

"It's a parliamentary debate; been around for hundreds of years."

"I heard you were a champion of that," he said.

"Yeah—but that's a whole other story."

Until then I'd only taught public speaking. Parliamentary debating was a natural progression. So I added a set of debating hints to the notes I'd already given the guys on how to make a speech.

Later on, a publisher turned those notes into a nifty little book. If you have an interest, you can pick it up on Amazon: *Talking Your Way to the Top: the nervous person's overnight guide to public speaking.*

Anyway, we ran that debate, and the guys wised up to the value of being able to present all sides of an argument, and delighted in doing just that.

And Kenny got the message, and quit on the idea of leading hoodlums.

And parliamentary debates became a regular and wildly popular feature in our class.

Return of the Prodigal

After getting out of Rikers and turning his life around, Kenny returned with me to Rikers, this time as a paid and respected instructor sharing Eagles principles.

Together we decided to do a reprise of that McDonald's debate, but, this time, upped the ante by recruiting a team of top outside pros to come in and debate the inmates.

Sensing some good publicity, the superintendent gave the okay for a camera crew to come in and make a movie of that event. He also okayed the editor of a monthly magazine that I was writing for to attend the debate and write it up.

Needless to say, the entire Rikers class got revved up.

In just a moment, we'll time travel back to Rikers to sit in on that debate. I think you'll be gob-smacked, especially by the weird reaction of a McDonald's bigwig.

"How could anyone be so dumb?" said Kenny.

I'll tell you all about that in a moment, after we attend the debate. Right now, let's show you what you see the moment you exit the prison gates.

INTO THE SUNLIGHT

The first thing you see is the rising sun. And three bright rings are wrapped around it. You see them in your mind's eye, right?

So, now, beneath the light of the sun, you see a mountain.

It's a mountain we've all got to climb.

It's WHAT we all have to do in life.

I'll be your guide as you climb that mountain.

But we'll do that in our next session.

Right now, let's focus on those three circles around the sun. They show HOW to get in shape to climb the mountain. We call them USA, Liberty, and SAM.

Easy to remember, right?

- *USA* to defang the snake;
- *Liberty* to emasculate the gremlin;
- and *SAM* to kill the witch.

USA

Let's begin with the snake that bit into your heart and created the *Wall of Emotional Damage.*

Here's question for you: *How can we heal a broken heart?*

Here's the answer given by New Yorker Dr. Albert Ellis. He was judged by his peers as the most helpful psychoanalyst of the 20th century. He coined the term, USA—*Unconditional Self Acceptance.* It means that we have to accept a simple fact:

> No matter what happened to you along the way, and
> no matter your crime, the self at the core of your being
> is perfect.

As children, we know this in our hearts.

But adults tell us differently and we come to doubt our value. We bow to the pressure of other people's opinions—loved ones and enemies, both—and accept that we are flawed and unworthy.

Let's hear Dr. Ellis talk about it. Here's the man himself:

> *Unconditional Self Acceptance means accepting
> yourself, your life, your aliveness, your enjoyments,
> what you want to do; avoiding what you <u>don't</u>
> want to do; with poor achievement as well as with
> good achievement. And it means accepting yourself
> with little approval or with no damned approval;
> accepting yourself when you know you're shnooky,
> and accepting yourself in a good environment or a
> crummy environment; with poor talents and abilities,
> and with just about no talents and abilities; with
> handicaps, stupidities, ugliness, weaknesses of body
> and mind, with poor finances, no matter what.
> That's what self acceptance is. You can always accept
> yourself. Now when you don't do this, you get shame,*

> *embarrassment, humiliation, feelings of inadequacy,*
> *lack of confidence, anxiety, depression, and self-pity.*

What I would add to Dr. Ellis's words is that the world has been around for millions of years and only the fittest have survived.

So every ancestor of yours was a survivor.

And *you're* the person they produced.

So congratulate yourself for that, because you've inherited what it takes to survive, and to pass that onto your children.

So, accept that you're human.

And that moods are normal.

They distinguish us from the animals.

So there's no need to get down on your *self* for having been a sleepwalker.

And every other person is a human, too.

So don't waste a moment resenting anyone who ever let you down—*they were driven by their own set of demons.*

Like the eagle, you're as worthy of being on the planet as any other creature.

Anyway, as Dr. Ellis made clear, 'worthy' is just an opinion. You are 'good' or 'deserving' because *you* think so.

Sure we all have *behaviors* that need attending to, but that's a whole other issue. And, as we'll see in a moment, adjusting habits can be both fun and painless.

When you have USA—and you can make a gift of it to yourself right now—you value yourself merely because you are alive and kicking.

For that reason alone you 'deserve' an enjoyable life—and can quit the crazy habit of getting down on your *self* for imagined defects.

So, tell that to your gremlin.

Liberty

Let's apply the second ring around the sun to shut that little devil down. That ring spells L-I-B-E-R-T-Y: *Liberty*. It's short for *Liberating Beliefs*.

So, the beginning of the end of the reign of your inner gremlin, is to replace *Imprisoning Beliefs with Liberating Beliefs*.

We already considered a couple of imprisoning beliefs:

> *I can't get what I need within the system—so it's okay*
> *to get what I want by cheating the system.*

Such beliefs get us through childhood, but as adults they get us into trouble.

And don't forget:

> *Your gremlin got released from jail at the same*
> *time you did. He's still lurking in your brain, and,*
> *now, more than ever, he's aching to reinforce those*
> *imprisoning beliefs, and he's desperate to enforce your*
> *poisoned losing psychic contract—the idea you bought*
> *into as a kid that you're destined to become a loser.*

Happily, now that you're awake to what's going on, *you can scrap that contract.*

Now—right here, this very moment—you can *get real.*

You do that by switching your mind-set from *No-Can-Do* to *Yes-I-can-do*. Here's the thing:

> *Beliefs are self-fulfilling, so if you believe it can't be*
> *done, or if you believe it can be done, you're right—*
> <u>*both times!*</u>

So replace '*I can't get what I need within the system*' with '*If I come up with a plan, hone my skills, and persevere, I can get whatever I realistically need.*'

That does NOT mean that you should become an undying optimist.

No!

Blind optimism leads to wishful thinking.

And wishful thinking always leads to trouble.

BUT

and listen up now because here comes another big idea:

> *Liberating beliefs blend a Can-Do attitude with realism, and create* <u>*PATHFINDERS*</u>.

SAM

A pathfinder sees and then *applies* the advice contained within that third ring around the sun.

It spells the letters, S-A-M—you see them right?

They stand for *Self-Affirming Maneuvers*.

Pathfinders replace *Self-Defeating-Behaviors* with *Self-Affirming Maneuvers*.

What does that mean, exactly? Glad you asked.

Buddha said "the wise man should make of himself an island that no flood may overcome."

The way to make that happen is to replace self-defeating behaviors with <u>S</u>elf-Affirming <u>M</u>aneuvers—<u>SAM</u>.

- It means <u>*actively*</u> *pursuing your own best interests.*
- It means consciously setting long-term goals, then setting milestones and going for them—one step at time, slowly but surely, steadily and relentlessly.

For openers, focus on acquiring, honing, and selling a marketable skill. Self-affirming maneuvers include showing up on time, and going the extra mile. And working on your people skills: smiling, sharing kind words, helping others, and, crucially, taking care of yourself—attending the gym not the tobacconist, that kind of thing.

So, *USA*, *Liberty*, and *SAM*.

- *USA* for your *heart*;
- *Liberty* for your *head*;
- and *SAM* for your *behaviors*.

I bet you know all this, already.

But let's be honest.

Sometimes things go off the rails.

> *Well, that is the precisely the moment for yet another self-affirming maneuver.*

Select an uplifting, liberating thought.

Intuition will shine a light on the way forward.

So, follow through with a daring leap of faith.

If the goal of life is to comfort each other and leave a meaningful legacy, then prison itself might be the best place on earth to practice some of those self-affirming maneuvers.

Your smile can bring out the sun.

Your kind word can ease a deep pain.

Your friendly gesture can dislodge a bullet and set a heart to healing.

THE BIG DAY

As promised, come share a taste of what went down at Rikers on the day of the McDonald's debate. Then I'll share some comments—good and bad—that I'm sure will catch your attention.

Right now, here's the promo:

> *Rikers Correctional Facility is the world's largest penal colony. Today, for the first time in a decade, a camera crew is allowed to enter the Rikers walls to document a head-to-head clash with Rikers inmates and a legal team led by top attorneys. But this battle will be fought with neither fists nor legal strategies, but with ideas.*

As they walked into the room, every member of the Rikers class was nervous.

The movie crew looked deadly serious.

The silver-headed magazine editor looked like a high court judge.

The smiling guest team—poised, confident, and immaculately dressed—clearly were big-time public speaking pros.

Our Rikers team had just barely figured out how it all worked. So the worry for us was that the day would turn into a rout.

Okay, then, so you can figure for yourself who the winner should have been, here's a snippet of what went down.

John Wareham Introduces the Debate

We meet here at Rikers to learn how to think about ideas. Some individuals say ideas are dangerous and that you should be very cautious about what you say, but we have learned enough, instead, no matter how outrageous idea might seem we can discuss it. A man here can express whatever view he wants, so long as he's able to defend it and listen to an opposing view. And that certainly holds true today as we debate the proposition, *It is Better to Rob a Bank than work at McDonald's*. I should point out that we are picking McDonald's only because it is the archetypal fast-food restaurant and employer.

For the guests, opening speaker Tovi Kratovil, a New York City courtroom attorney, used a poem to frame the real-world case for bank robbery.

Emile (Tovi) Kratovil. Guest

Our topic is straightforward: "It is better to rob a bank than work at McDonald's." I want to define the terms by which we prepared to support this proposition. We're talking about individuals with limited options and we're talking about the difficulty in finding a way off of the limitations on those options we're talking about the real world; we're talking the real options; we're talking about the segment of the population that has been once or multiple times in prison . . . If you succeed in getting a job, it's a minimum wage job; it can support rent, food, or the monthly needs of an individual, a family. And if you do succeed in achieving it you have job security, few or no benefits, little or no hope of a raise. If you apply a purely logical, rational analysis to whether it is better to rob a bank or work at McDonald's, and if you want some money to run your life, and if you want independence, and you want hope of getting ahead, I think that like the great Willie Sutton, you rob that bank. This anonymous refrain sums it up. I'm not a rap speaker but I give it to you for the logic as well as for the emotion:

> My mother goes to work cold- bustin' her ass.
> My sister's cute but she's got no gear.
> Three pairs of pants with my brother I share.
> Then at school, see I made a fool.
> With one and a half pairs of pants, it ain't cool.
> But there's no dollars for nothing else.
> I've got beans, bread, and rice on my shelf.
> Every day I see my mother struggling.
> Now it's time. I got to do something.
> I look for work, I get dissed like a jerk.
> I do odd jobs and come home like a slob.

So here comes Rob, his goal is shimmering.
He gives 200 for a quick delivering.
Now there's steak with the beans and rice.
The family's happy: everything is new.
Now, tell me what the eff am I supposed to do?

Yeah, that's the problem, don't yah think? Cliff opened the case for the Rikers team with an equally practical point.

Clifton Powell. Rikers Team

The average of a bank robbery is $20,000—not much money. If and when you get caught you will get at least 15 years in prison. Compare that with working at McDonald's. You may not have many skills at the beginning but that's what McDonald's does: gives you skills, so you can become a corporate chef. You can go back to school. McDonald's has options. The old days are over. When Bonnie and Clyde robbed banks, they went in and robbed the whole bank. They went into the safe. They went into people's pockets. They took everything. Nowadays when you rob a bank you only rob one teller. And when you rob that teller, you usually get only get $2000 or $3000. You spend that pretty quick on the fast life. Then what do you do? You've got to rob another bank. And never forget, even the great bank robber Willie Sutton got caught.

And, now, Tom Morgan, a radio broadcaster, and, as became clear, a wealthy Smith Barney investment manager, took center stage.

Tom Morgan. Guest

Life is a series of decisions where you weigh the odds. For most crimes committed in America, only something like 15 percent of the perpetrators ever get into jail. So if you rob a bank, the odds are in your favor . . . We live in a capitalist society, which means you've got to have capital. Capital ain't six bucks an hour. Capital is 100 grand, which you can get from robbing a bank. I'm in the investment business, so I've got to advise people about odds all the time. If a guy came to me and said, 'Should I put my money on this guy who is going to work for McDonald's or on him—he's going to rob a bank.' I'd say—'Him! Him! The odds favor the robber. That's a better investment. Let's go with the odds.' Go-with-the-odds.

Yeah, Tom. Very funny. Jonathan, a shy and intense guy who worked his way onto the Rikers team was next.

Jonathan Hutchinson. Rikers Team

We heard a lot of words today. Words like logic, education, limited options, compassion, victimless crime, and playing the odds. But nobody said *Better*. And I'm going to tell you that's the key word this morning. We're not really talking about robbing a bank; we're talking about doing something with the limited options available to us. I love basketball. Some of the greatest players worked at McDonald's. Magic Johnson turned the whole game of basketball around, but he had a job at McDonald's first. Julius Irving took the basketball game to a whole other level, but he had a job at McDonald's first. We're talking about being better able to help children who are the real innocent victims of the society we live in. We're talking about being better able to support the economic institution that we are a part of, whether we know it or not. We're talking about being part of a group of people, a community of humanity. We've *got* to be better right?

Hey! Well done, Jonathan. Next came the urbane, silver-tongued, criminal attorney, John McLean, sometime chief of a major Hong Kong law firm.

John McLean. Guest

Working in McDonald's for ten hours a day, being ordered around every few minutes by rude and thoughtless people who regard you only as a robot without feelings? How can that possibly compare with working only a *few* hours and ending the day not with a hundred dollars in your pocket but with *thousands*? Now I would like to talk to you about the victimless crime. Let's look at what it's like for the banks. Here is this girl, the teller. You come up to her. You've charmed her with your smile. There are no guns involved, just pure charm. You say to her, 'Your life is worth more than that canvas bag, so hand it over.' She hands over the canvas bag and she smiles at you. The fact is, that she has lost *nothing*. Compare that, gentlemen, with the thought of robbing a girl of her virginity. She can never get that back once you have taken it. But the bank is something different. Even though you've stolen its money, more money will come in again. It's like an ever-filling pitcher. It's no problem at all for the bank. Basically no one gets hurt—and *you* get a good deal of satisfaction. As my ending parable, let's say it's a bit like the result you might get if you had the opportunity of squeezing a rich man's testicles. It hurts, it hurts—but there is no permanent damage.

Yeah, kinda funny, right? But, now, Berry, looking every inch the Golden Gloves contender that he used to be, set that argument onto the back foot.

Herbert Berry. Rikers Team

No permanent damage? I think Mr. McLean would be singing a different tune if I—or anybody in this room—put a crush on *his* testicles. Now I would like to ask you a question: what if your son or your daughter came to you and said, 'Dad, I'm thinking about robbing a bank. Should I do that, or get a job at McDonald's? What should I do?' Would you tell your child, 'Yes, child, yes, just go and rob the bank, you might do well.' Mr. McLean was talking about being ordered around in McDonald's and the manager telling you, do this, do that. But ask yourself: would you rather for him to tell you that, knowing you can go home after working your shift, or would you rather be here at Rikers with the officers ordering you around, knowing that you can't go home, knowing that you have to do what they say? I know right now, that if I had an option to work at McDonald's today, even with that manager ordering me around, I'd take it. *However you perceive your reality to be, that's what your future will be.* If you perceive yourself as a person whose only option is robbing a bank, then that's what your future will be—*in jail. Adversity makes a man look at himself.* When you look in the mirror at yourself, what do you want to see? When other people look at you, what do you want *them* to see? Do you want them to see an upstanding young man that's trying to do something with himself, trying to better his life? Or do you want them to see a *thug*? For me, that's no option. Frankly, I don't think there's even anything to talk about.

The Debate was unanimously awarded to the Rikers team. Herbert Berry was awarded best speaker.

Afterthoughts

I was happy with the result, as was our timekeeper, Jerome. Here's what he said:

> Yeah, the right team won. The guests were great, but they didn't understand that if you're just getting out of prison and you got no prospects, robbery ain't just a funny idea. It's a real choice. But robbing a bank ain't victimless. The odds might be in your favor, but the stakes are your life. Fail and you're either dead or back in jail, big-time. And even if you win you lose. 'Cos you don't get no self-respect. And now you're a poster boy for racial profiling. The Rikers team argued for dignity, what you're calling USA, right? They said McDonald's was a stepping stone—so that's a liberating belief, right? And what about SAM? They said humble actions create great citizens—that's self affirming maneuvers? Am I right, or am I right?

If you haven't already listened in to the debate, you can see the video at the Eagles website. If you have seen it you'll have joined me in asking, who would ever have believed that any of these Rikers guys had never spoken in public until they landed in this Eagles class?

And think about these next comments after the debate, this time from members of the guest team:

Tovi Kratovil: *The thing that struck me most intimately, most emotionally, were the several moments when I saw on the faces of several in the audience, and even on the speakers, that flash of recognition that comes when you begin to realize that it's possible to do something that you didn't think you could do.*

John McLean: *I was astounded by their grace and skill. Not only when the debate team began to speak, but even as they and the rest of the Rikers class walked into the room.*

RIPPLE EFFECTS—GOOD AND NOT-SO-MUCH

I promised to explain how my answer to Kenny had a ripple effect that never stopped.

For openers, as you know, Kenny became a Rikers instructor and changed the lives of countless young men.

Then the McDonald's guest team debate—including the full text—got written up as the cover story in that national glossy, *The Journal of the Conference Board*. Berry's photo graced the cover, and the article showcased the fact that prisons contained men of untapped talent.

We posted that article and the video on the Eagles website, and the publicity from it inspired other prisons to consider debating programs.

BUT—*but but, but . . .*

Despite the fact that the guys in green won the debate by making superb arguments *for* McDonald's, and the write-up was dream publicity for them, I got a call from a very distressed magazine editor. Some big-wig zombie in that fast-food empire was offended by the magazine article, and was demanding the firing of the hapless scribe. For sure, the next issue carried a personal apology from the editor for the highly favorable write up.

De-press-ing.

Well, sad to say, after I moved up to Downstate, parliamentary debating disappeared from all Rikers programs.

But wait!

Because many people read about the event or saw the

video, more than ten years later, prison debating made a comeback. Indeed, that reinvention of the wheel we created got written up in the *New York Times*, where the tacit assumption of the piece was that parliamentary debating was the key to reforming criminals.

But, uh, no! I beg to differ.

The Big Mistake

Those who believed that parliamentary debating cures criminality were like the so-called 'Wise Blind Men of Indostan'.

Using touch alone, they became so focused on trunk and skin, tusk and tail that none of them realized that these were parts of just *one* animal—an elephant.

So, too, parliamentary debating is just one part of the life-altering Eagles regimen.

The elephant itself is KNOWLEDGE—*new* knowledge.

Truly understanding the 4-Walls model is key to releasing inmates of mental prisons.

Reading up on those ideas, seeing movies about them, discussing them, writing poems about them, and debating them, all of which we did in prison, are merely *methods* for getting that model across.

It is the Big Ideas inside those walls that transform us.

So, where did the grace of all the guys in green, even as they entered the debate room, come from?

It was the end-product of their having invested the time and effort to share and absorb the over-arching model. Getting hold of that big idea conveyed an inner peace and outward grace that was there to be seen before anyone spoke a word.

At that point, everyone was well and truly aware of the 4-Walls model.

As I'm hoping you are now, too.

You're a survivor, right?

So the next step is to become a *pathfinder*.

In this post-Covid 19 world your job is to join the ranks of the countless Eagles graduates who went on to become happy, productive, fulfilled citizens.

You've gotten yourself ready for that climb by sighting the wisdom with the three rings around the rising sun:

USA—*Unconditional Self Acceptance*;

Liberty—*Liberating Beliefs*;

and SAM—*Self-Affirming Maneuvers*.

So, next session we'll guide you as you set out to climb the sunlit mountain you now face.

We call it *Independence Mountain*.

Way off in the sky, you'll catch sight of a star, too.

Tell you all about it in our next chapter.

How to Scale a Mountain

Tread Wisely, and Rest Along the Way

Getting arrested, cuffed, and delivered to the New York City Tombs was humiliating. What happened in my tiny underground, overnight cell lies at the heart of the *The Breakout Plan*—and the message I'll share with you now.

But first, consider the beginning—or maybe the end—of a related journey by my good friend Omar:

> *I've been in prison so long that I don't have anyone waiting for me on the outside. And, when I get out next month I don't have anywhere to stay either. But I do have a plan. I'll head straight to a homeless shelter, and stay there . . .*

Before he tells you how that worked out, let's do a lightning recap.

Box Circle Triangle

Like I already said, this Eagles Breakout Plan is *not* a simple plan.

But you're still with me, so you're clearly up for the challenge. So let's do a mental exercise and see if we can make it *unforgettable*—and at journey's end, we'll see if we succeeded.

So, now, go to the blackboard in the back of your mind—we've all got one, right? Grab an imaginary piece of chalk, and, using four lines—one on the bottom, one on each side, and one on the top—draw a square box.

One . . . two . . . three . . . four lines. That was easy, right?

Now, next to the box draw a circle.

And next to that circle draw a triangle.

Now take a hard look, and burn those three images into your brain.

Square, Circle, Triangle—you got it, right?

Now, inside the square box write *Prison*.

Inside the circle write *Sun*.

Inside the triangle write *Mountain*.

The Box

Okay then. That square box is the mental prison you just released yourself from.

The sun showed HOW to prepare for the journey to come.

And climbing that mountain is WHAT we've got to do now.

You remember that every mental prison has four walls, right?

- That bottom line is the *Wall of Emotional Damage*— snakebite suffered that created a set of beliefs that gets us through childhood BUT which lock into:

- The line on your left, being the *Wall of Imprisoning Beliefs*—which comes with an nasty inner gremlin who reinforces negative opinions beliefs and enforces a loser's psychic contract, which now locks us into:-

- The line on the top, being the *Wall of Self-Defeating Behaviors*, driven by a seductive witch who leaves us for dead.

- The line on your right, is the *Wall of the Illusion of Choice*—the zombie-like blindness of a sleepwalker that prevents you from waking up to what's been getting you into trouble.

The Door

Happily, there's a door in the middle of that last wall—*The Door of Understanding*. It was invisible to you before, but now you've seen it. And now you've passed through it.

So, no matter whether you're inside a real concrete and steel prison right now, you know why you also used to be in a mental prison.

So now you're a free spirit.

You passed through the door of understanding, and stepped out of your four-walled mental prison,

In our last session you saw the rising sun—and the three bright rings wrapped around it.

They showed HOW to get in shape to climb the mountain. We called them USA, Liberty, and SAM.

USA to defang the snake, *Liberty* to emasculate the gremlin, and *SAM* to kill the witch.

- USA—*Unconditional Self Acceptance*;
- Liberty—*Liberating Beliefs*;
- and SAM—*Self-affirming Maneuvers*.

And now, in the light of that golden sun, you see a lush green mountain: the *Mountain of Independence*.

- It's a mountain we've all got to climb.
- It's WHAT we all have to do in life.

There's also an invisible WHY—a reason that the Breakout Plan works, and I'll share that soon.

Checkup Time

Meantime, just to make sure that our Box, Circle, Triangle model really is unforgettable:

- Close your eyes and envisage a box.
- You were trapped inside it.
- You got out of the box and saw a circle—*the sun.*
- It told you HOW to prepare for a big climb.
- And now you're looking at a triangle—*a mountain.*
A mountain we've all got to climb. It's WHAT we have to do.
- Box—Circle—Triangle.
- Prison—Sun—Mountain
- Trapped, Buffed, and Free.

Free to climb Independence Mountain—*right now!*

Okay, here we go!

INDEPENDENCE MOUNTAIN

Let's begin with this poem delivered by Sheldon in our Downstate class:

> *Searching for my soul in the mirror*
> *I see a ghost of the boy who was free*
> *And on his shoulder*
> *the guiding hands of the man*
> *that prison has made me.*

The lesson's clear, right? *It's time to put away childish things, and man-up.* As Dr. Carl Jung, a father of modern psychology, puts it:

> *Life summons us to Independence. To fail to heed this call is to become ensnared and to invent increasingly valid reasons to run from life while remaining imprisoned within the morally poisonous atmosphere of infancy.*

So let's get real, and set about scaling Independence Mountain.

The Three Plateaus

You can see that mountain in your mind's eye right now. It has one . . . two . . . three plateaus:

At the bottom is the *Table of Bread*;

above that is the *Field of Dreams*;

at the top is the *Haven of Love*.

The Table of Bread. The Field of Dreams. The Haven of Love. You see them right?

That mountain looks daunting. How will you ever manage to climb it?

The answer to that question lies right beneath your feet.

You didn't see it before but now you do.

You're standing smack in the middle of a garden: the *Garden of Gifts*—your gifts.

Let's talk about those gifts.

THE GARDEN OF GIFTS

First, you are indeed a survivor; the product of millions of years of evolution. You've arrived in the world with incredible talents and gifts. The immediate challenge is to turn those gifts into survival skills.

We think of gifts as innate talents.

But stay with me now, because *our gifts may also include apparent flaws and failings.*

A great weakness may force us to look inside ourselves and develop a hidden strength.

Aesop, an ancient Greek slave, was runty, squint-eyed, liver-lipped, potbellied, and bandy. But he tapped an underlying gift, and blinded his listeners to what some said were loathsome looks, by telling them stories—

which thereby earned him a living and respect, and, finally, his freedom.

I could identify with that, because, as you may know, a nasty stutter led me to attempt suicide. Happily I survived and took up public speaking to overcome my stutter. I became a national oratory and debating champion, then earned a handsome living as a keynote speaker.

The celebrated actor, James Earl Jones, another reformed stutterer, found a similar gift.

Untapped Gifts

In fact, many of our troubles arise from unused faculties.

> *So, getting into trouble may be a sign that we're doing something right!*

As a schoolboy, Malcolm X dreamed of becoming a lawyer. But his teacher said—his words, not mine— 'That's no job for a nigger,' and Malcolm quit on his dream and became a criminal. And then discovered an infinitely greater vocation inside prison. And his spirit has never died.

My stutter also resulted in stints as a juvenile delinquent that led to my arrest. But, half a lifetime later, that turned out to be a gift. I could sense and share the pain with any inmate anywhere. It's why I'm talking to you right now.

And the fact you've tuned in to listen is telling me that you have an untapped gift.

I don't know what it is. Maybe you don't either.

But it will show up.

And when it does, you'll see that you've been on a journey, and, as we'll see later, that it may well have been your guide.

Speaking of which, here's a message from my great friend, Eagles leader, Hassan Gale:

> For years, anger and confusion blocked my ability to think constructively. My mind was a hellish mental prison. Fellow inmates confided the same torment. So, I eventually convinced an open-minded programs officer to try something new. That's how John and the Eagles' program to came to state prisons. And, now, I was on a journey, learning to dismantle mental prisons, and tapping into forgotten talents and dormant inner gifts. After my release John asked me to help lead the Eagles in New York City. "It takes an ex-offender to render an offender and ex," he said. Yeah, right! To be free we must not always have been free—and only a former inmate can truly liberate a prisoner still in one. If this sounds like something that you can relate to, check out our website. Anything that you'd like to share there about our program would be both welcomed and appreciated.—Peace.

THE TABLE OF BREAD

So, now that we've considered the notion of the gifts we didn't know we had, let's think about the first plateau—the *Table of Bread*.

Here's an Aesop story you might like.

> 'I have a whole bag of tricks and countless ways of escaping my enemies, the dogs,' bragged a fox to a cat. 'Gosh I've only got one trick,' said the cat. 'I wish you could teach me some of yours.' The fox looked doubtful. 'Maybe one day I'll teach you a couple of my easier dodges,' he said.
>
> Suddenly, a yelping a pack of hounds came rushing

*towards them. The cat instantly scampered up a tree
and disappeared in the foliage. 'This is my only trick,'
she called down to the fox. Which one are you going
to use?' After contemplating his many tricks, the fox
decided to make a run for it. But too late! The dogs
were upon him. And that was the end of the fox,
bagful of tricks and all.*

While we're thinking about the moral of that story, let me
share part of a speech to an Eagles graduating class by my
friend and Eagles co-founder, the late great Joe Roberts.

Joe's Journey

*When I got out of jail my Ivy League degree in
literature didn't get me a job. So I took a job
scrubbing pots in a Harlem kitchen. It came with
two meals a day and a wage—enough for me to rent
a room. I was self-sufficient, and grateful and proud
to be so. I figured I was on a journey, and would do
whatever it took for as long as it took. I scrubbed
those pots for six months and I always gave it my best.
Those pots had never looked so shiny. I also attended
the local church and worked on their local projects.
Not because I'm religious, but because everyone in
that community understood my situation, and was
proud to support me. I needed that.*

So, now, let me share my take on Aesop's cat and fox fable.

To me, the moral is that the cat tapped into its gifts and
honed one unique survival skill that always worked.

So let's copy the cat.

The trick we need is an unfailing skill and expertise that
other people will gladly pay us for. A skill we can take to
market.

One such skill, at the bottom of the food chain—literally—is scrubbing pots and pans. But there's dignity in *every* job, no matter how humble, so that can be a great place to earn a living.

But mere survival isn't enough.

We need to nourish the heart as well as the body. We need *inner* growth. We need recreation.

We need to *re*-create our *selves*.

So let's about the next plateau—the *Field of Dreams*.

THE FIELD OF DREAMS

You might want to pursue a hobby or a sport. Or read some great books. Or write or paint, or play a musical instrument, or follow or join a band. Or, as with Joe, you may want to contribute to the community around you.

And remember, humans are psychologically programed to do favors for people who do favors for us. So working a second job for free can also be a way to get ahead in life.

- Becoming a counselor and helping young people avoid your mistakes might be one way to head down that route.

- And political campaigns are always looking for volunteers.

Either way you'll meet go-getters and make new friends. And a new upbeat life may come your way.

Dollops of Dollars

Or, you might just want to acquire, hone, and sell a skill that earns a better paycheck.

If so, then, like Joe, *aim to be the best in the world in what you do*. That's easier than it sounds.

- Create a narrow niche for yourself in your own

backyard.

- Become the neighborhood *go-to guy*—the person known to have the specific skill to solve a specific tricky problem.

Never forget there's only one of you.

Fulfillment comes in expressing the real you.

A sense of purpose sometimes flashes into consciousness.

So, incorporate that purpose into your regular life. And, advance towards your goals every day.

Words Can Work Magic

And remember this:

> *We cannot always control the racing of an anxious heart, or the spinning of a fretful mind. But we can always control what we say—and what we say can change our situations.*

I'll share some lines that can help you achieve just that in a moment. Right now, let's visit the Haven of Love.

THE HAVEN OF LOVE

Prison removes the outer shell and reveals the inner spirit. On arrival, the inmate is stripped of his clothes, showered of his dignity, and assigned a uniform that bears his new identity, being a number. And, in the moment he enters his concrete cell and the iron door closes behind him, he discovers what we all must learn:

> *We're all alone in this together, and we gotta survive somehow.*

Visiting Day

A visit from a loved one is the surest sign that someone cares, that one's feelings of loss, longing, and love are shared.

No matter what an eavesdropper may hear, the underlying pain of those who meet within prison walls is always evident. Big Bear can tell you all about it:

> *Even after all these years*
> *visiting day, I must say,*
> *can leave me in tears.*
> *To see loved ones I first strip naked*
> *and consent to be degraded.*
> *Needless to say*
> *to embrace the faces*
> *who journey the day*
> *to this cold chalet*
> *come in answer*
> *to what I pray.*
> *Being with those I love is joy*
> *but too soon time flies,*
> *then comes goodbye.*

Hutch tells of the visit itself:

> *On this day, I look my best;*
> > *fresh dressed, nicely pressed,*
> > *hair sharp, beard tight.*
> > *A dab of cologne? No contest.*
>
> *A C.O. slips me my guest room pass.*
> *I'm out the door, gone—loved ones await.*
> *Hugs and kisses, I miss you so much.*
> *Hands soft to the touch caress my face,*
> *and my mind drifts to another place.*
>
> *Look how much the kids have grown.*
> *Boyyee, you been working out?*
> > *Your muscles showing!*
> > *Maybe a little.*

Nephew's on my lap,
> *I tickle,*
> *he wiggles,*
> *we all giggle.*
Sis's eyes swell with tears,
I wish you were at home, she says.
> *In that second,*
> *I truly felt alone.*

Kindred Spirits

Like most other creatures we look around for kindred spirits, as did Eagles graduate Andre Rivera is this next excerpt from *How to Survive a Bullet to the Heart:*

> *While incarcerated I've learned to be passive and humble—and observant. Two sayings I go by:*
> - *Keep your head above water and watch out for the sharks.*
> - *And cut the lawn grass short to expose the snakes.*
> *You know who your friends are when you're locked up. A stranger you meet here can wind up being your best friend for life. And the best friend you grew up with out there is really the stranger.*

All too often, believing that others exclude us, we suffer, 'the illusion of exclusion.' Andre explains it:

> *The only thing that separates us is each other. Just look at our backgrounds. Minorities from ghettoes raised by a single parent and grew up around drugs, prostitutes, guns, and violence.*
> *But if we educate each other and stop with the racism, we can fix the crazy laws and sentencing guidelines that got most of us here in the first place— and are holding too many of us here right now. That's what I've learned.*

Kinds of Love

The Greeks have a wonderful word for the human love that we can see around us every day: AGAPE.

The corrections officer who shares a smile and a kind word. The fellow inmate who shares a thumbs up. These gestures of human connectedness acknowledge that we are, indeed, under the skin brothers and sisters.

Prison life is full of this kind of love.

The moral though, is that *the way to have a friend, is to be a friend.*

Countless people asked me why I was attracted to prison teaching. The answer is easy. I met so many intelligent, empathetic people. Our discussions had a life-changing effect—on me as much as them. I valued their appreciation for what I did, as mutual respect and *agape.*

THE MESSAGE

Let's hear what happened to my great friend Omar.

> *Yeah, well I got a job as an air-conditioning installer. And, after a year on the job, they put me in charge of running a team. But they didn't increase my hourly rate. I'd still be there, if they'd done that. Instead I decided to set up my own aircon consulting business and recruit my own team. That worked out great. So in my spare time I'm indulging my passion for creating abstract art—and I've sold some of my pieces, too.*

As you see, Omar got the message—all of it. So let's do a lightning recap to make sure that the model is burned into your brain, too.

- Box—Circle—Triangle.
- Prison—Sun—Mountain

You remember that, right?

So close your eyes and envisage a four-sided box.

You were trapped inside it.

Your companions were . . .

> *a snake, yes;*
> *a gremlin, yes;*
> *a witch, yes;*
> *and a . . . zombie–right?*

And what were the four walls?

> Yes it's all coming back, right?

> > *Emotional Damage;*
> > *Imprisoning Beliefs;*
> > *Self-Defeating Behaviors;*
> > and, of course,
> > the *Illusion of Choice.*

You escaped through the *Door of Understanding,* got out of the box and saw a circle–the *sun.*

Three rings around it–USA, Liberty, and SAM– told you HOW to get fit for a big climb. .

- USA–*Unconditional Self Acceptance;*
- Liberty–*Liberating Beliefs;*
- and SAM–*Self Affirming Maneuvers.*

And then you saw a triangle–a mountain, with three plateaus:

- the *Table of Bread;*
- the *Field of Dreams;*
- and the *Haven of Love.*

And now you know how to climb that mountain, right?

But wait. There's more.

Superstar

Tilt your head to the sky.

Way, way off in the blue there's a twinkling star. It's a guiding star—a *polestar*.

As if in a secret code it is signaling you to fulfill your mission on this planet. To do that, you'll have to tap your deepest gift. And maybe right now that gift looks like a failing. Maybe it's why you landed in jail.

> Kenny Johnson wound up there because he was a violent stickup man with a drug habit. Joe, was a thief and a coke addict. My stutter led me to suicide and delinquency. Yet the three of us decided that our purpose in life—our star—was to help guys in prison, or on their way in or out of one. That became a guiding star.

Your star will be related to *your* gift. For sure, winding up on drugs or in prison is telling you that you're not using all your talents. An Eagles retreat might be the tonic you need. You can check that out our website.

THE WHY

As mentioned, there's a hidden reason for why the Breakout Plan works.

When we truly commit to the program we engage a mysterious phenomenon called synchronicity.

Synchronicity: Carl Jung coined the word, then quantum scientists confirmed that marvel.

It's the *opposite* of a mere coincidence.

> *Synchronicity is when two related events happen at the same time precisely because forces in the universe— and inside our hearts and minds—make them happen.*

Time and again, the stranger I've needed to help me solve a problem has suddenly appeared—then changed my life.

In the moment of meeting, I sense that the universe has brought us together.

It may well be why you're listening right now.

I promised some lines—affirmations, actually—that you could speak to help you change your situation. But first, let's revisit my overnight cell in the Manhattan Tombs.

> I got arrested, allegedly for jumping a turnstile. Cuffed behind my back, I was paraded on Broadway, tossed into a paddywagon, booked, then ushered into a tiny cell with 18 other overnight inmates. I needed something to distract me. Happily, I'd been allowed to keep my paperback copy of Shakespeare's sonnets. As I flicked it open my gaze fell onto the first line of Sonnet number 74:
>
> *But be contented when that fell arrest without all bail shall carry thee away . . .*
>
> Wow—*synchronicity!* William Shakespeare himself was talking to me. I repeated the line, and the world slowed down. Then I knelt, jammed myself into a space beneath an iron bunk and enjoyed a peaceful night's sleep on a bare concrete floor.

So, right now, as promised, for when things seem to be going wrong for you, here's a life-altering self-affirming maneuver to whisper :

> *I am harmonious, poised and magnetic;*
> *my power is the force of the universe*
> *and the universe makes a way for me*
> *where there is no way that I can see.*

You can download several pages of such affirmations free from the eagles website.

Right now, as you set out to scale Independence Mountain, here's a thought from the German philosopher Goethe:

> *When we commit ourselves, providence moves too. A whole stream of events issues from that decision, raising in one's favor all manner of unforeseen incidents and meetings and material assistance, which no man could have dreamed would have come his way. Whatever you can do, or dream you can do, begin it. Boldness has genius, power, and magic in it. Begin it now.*

Or as we Eagles like to say:

> *Here's a word to the wise;*
> *keep your eyes on the prize*
> *for the lower we fall*
> *the higher we can rise.*

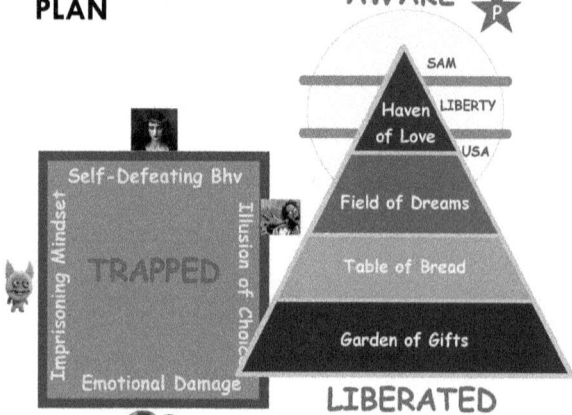

What If You Stumble?

The Way of the Pathfinder

I'm hoping that, in spite of the episodes we've already shared, after you got released from prison, you didn't get grabbed and shipped back behind the wall yet again. But if you did, then good news is on the way.

I'm guessing you got sucked into the pool of quicksand just outside the prison gate. So, for the next time out of those iron gates, I'm going to share some hard-won tips on how to sidestep that swamp.

Juvenile Delinquent

First, though, for reasons that'll soon become obvious, I need to confess that when I was ten years old I got arrested for breaking into a hotel and stealing a wallet. My father showed up to claim me from the local sergeant. But that sheriff was reluctant to release me from his office unless my father promised appropriate punishment.

"Yes," said my Dad. "I'll take him home and give him a hiding."

"So do it here now," said the enforcer. He slid his thick leather belt from his trousers and passed it to my father, who stood, lash in hand.

"So bend over, Jonny," he said. Then he delivered a sufficient bunch of lashes to my butt and bare legs to sate the sergeant. But the only change to me was a distrust and loathing for authority. My career as a petty larcenist continued with even more fervor.

Second Chance Challenges

Forty-five years later I was invited to create and teach a personal development program to prison inmates at Rikers Island.

At that time, after they were released, 80 percent of Rikers inmates returned inside three months. Wow! I made a vow to myself. I would bring that recidivism rate down, or I would quit.

I'll let my great friend, Richard Habersham, a contender for US Congress, share how that worked out:

> I was there on the graduation day at Downstate
> Prison, in the jam-packed library when the inmates
> presented John with a surprise thank you card they'd
> created. On the front was a cartoon drawing of John
> at a lectern. A balloon above his head spelled out his
> words, 'The graduates from my program go home and
> stay home.' Inside, the card was filled from edge to edge
> with heartfelt handwritten inmate tributes. John had
> been teaching there for ten years. The word was out.
> Those guys knew, better than absolutely anyone, that
> no Downstate Eagles graduate had ever returned.

A Crazy Plan?

How did we get to that point? Well, I have to confess that the belting I received as a kid had taught me that a change in behavior couldn't be *inflicted*.

By my reckoning, *all prisons were mental prisons*. We have to be transformed from the inside out; *change has to begin in the mind, and settle in the heart.*

I picked up on the advice of pioneering psychologist Carl Jung:

> The patient begins to get better when he truly
> understands his predicament; only then can he see a
> way out of it.

Yeah, right. The predicament was *the syndrome of serial incarceration.*

If you knew why you kept on winding up in prison you could change your thinking and escape your mental prison.

Experience had also taught me that *we only pay attention to the things that we discover for ourselves.*

So I decided to make each session a journey of discovery. I introduced discussion readings on the biggest life-changing ideas of modern psychology. And blended them with the brightest insights from the likes of of Plato and Shakespeare, and Martin Luther King Jr. and Spike Lee.

Then we—my earnest self and the now very upbeat guys in green—drove the messages home with public speaking and parliamentary debating.

Officials thought I was crazy. These criminals will never understand this stuff, they said. They sure got that wrong. In fact, it is easier to pick up on a big idea than a small one.

Everything came together. It built confidence and a couple of highly marketable skills: critical thinking, and the ability to communicate calmly and logically with anyone in any setting.

In fact, any inmate could quit at any point during the 13 weekly sessions. And, yes, we lost some guys along the way. But graduates gave the class a perfect score for both presentation and practicality. We seemed to getting somewhere.

Or maybe not.

Doubting Thomas

Thomas pulled me aside in a Rikers corridor.

"I love this class," he said. "And I see where you're going. You're showing how we've been, uh, affected, uh, damaged even, you said. And I get that. You said we gotta fix our, uh, situations, and you showed us how to do that—and I get that, too. Trouble is I just don't think I can make your ideas work for me. I'm in a tougher place than you can know. I mean you're a white guy in a good place or you wouldn't have the time to be out here. My problem used to be alcohol. I gave that up in here, but that don't change my situation back home. I work hard, but I got a family and kids and bills to pay. I'm hoping I can get it all back together. My wife's not so sure. Unless I, uh, go outside the system, there's no way I can make my situation work."

His eyes were clear and he was fit, so he'd probably invested time in the gym. His voice was soft and sincere. He wasn't asking for favors. He just wanted me to agree with him. And maybe I should have. Maybe he was one hundred percent right.

What to say? How should I respond to my Doubting Thomas?

"You're right, Thomas. I truly don't know your situation, and you're a thoughtful guy so I'm going to agree with you." He beamed. "But maybe it's something we both need to think about."

He stepped into the corridor, leaving me to ponder our exchange. I'd agreed that I didn't know his situation, which was true, and, also probably true, that he'd been doing his best. But his best had landed him in prison and now he was seeking advice. So, shouldn't I have offered him something better than what I just did? But like what? It was a puzzle.

I finally figured it out, and I'll share what I should have said to Thomas in a moment.

The Pool of Quicksand

First, though, let's take a peek at the quicksand just outside the prison gate.

As a motor cyclist I learned that 60 percent of motorcycle accidents happen in the first three months of owning the bike. And that 50 percent of such pileups happen within 800 yards of one's home.

So, one moral, I think, is that you're at serious risk during the first three months of stepping out of jail and embarking on a new life—and, nowhere more so than inside your own neck of the woods.

Bear in mind that in the moment of walking out the gate, there's a pool of quicksand in the form of:

- Local police officers. They've been alerted to your release; they know your criminal history, where you live, and what you look like.

- As they'd see it, they'd be derelict in their duty if they didn't make checking out anyone who just got out of jail a priority—especially a sophisticated repeat offender. And, of course, they have quotas to fill.

THREE UNHAPPY ROADS

So let's talk about two roads—the *Fast Track Back*, and the *Dead End Shoulder*—that lead good guys back to prison; then the *Crooked Shortcut* delivers dedicated bad guys into Hades.

After that we'll think about a way forward that'll get you going home and staying home.

The Fast Track Back

The fast way to take the *Fast Track Back* is to discount danger. So, maybe you talk to a drug dealer and catch the attention of a surly cop. Or, maybe, perhaps for a good reason, you miss a parole hearing. Suddenly, you're in that quicksand up to your armpits. Officialdom plucks you from the muck, delivers you back behind the wall, cleans you up with a cold shower, fits you with a fresh green suit, and locks you into a cold concrete cell. Most guys who come back inside three months get sucked into that swamp. My great friend Dwayne Speight, whom I met in my earliest days at Rikers, is happy to share his journey through that quagmire.

> People thought I was a cold-hearted bully, but I was sensitive and I wanted to help people. I was a quick learner, but my father wasn't around and I was too much of a handful for my mother.
>
> I looked for the easy way to get what I wanted from life, but compared to others I always seemed to come up short financially, so I fell into dealing drugs and petty larceny.
>
> I first got sent to jail when I was sixteen. I was scared of being locked up then. But I got used to it. When I got out I kept on doing drugs and selling drugs and stealing, and I wound up in jail several times. Then I added assault to one of my deals, and got a lengthier sentence.
>
> Even while serving that time, I sincerely believed that if I improved my criminal skills, that when I got out of jail I could make a good living doing more of the same at a higher level, and stay out of the clutches of the law.

Yeah, *that's* the problem: failing to realize that the odds against pulling off a crime are greater than ever; returning to same old people, places, and things—then coming back, this time with a longer sentence to serve.

The Dead-End Shoulder

The *Dead-End Shoulder* is the path taken by the 'almost persuaded' recidivist who leaves prison saying that he'll 'try to shoulder his responsibilities' by doing 'the right thing.' And that may well be his intention.

Alas, his criminal record makes it just about impossible to get a job, so he winds up doing something he detests for miserable pay and long hours. He wins praise from his probation officer, but his work days are hell and his home life is purgatory.

He's like a blinkered harnessed draught horse. But he's not a horse. He's a man. So, one gray day he raises a fist to the sky and says, *Fuck it!* And, in that moment, he feels gloriously excited and free. Then he follows through on his 'decision' to indulge the witchy wiles of drugs and criminality.

But the euphoria fades, bad karma follows, and all too soon he wakes up back behind the wall where he began—but, again, infinitely worse off than before.

The Crooked Shortcut

But what about the guy who joins up with a gang, stays clean himself, becomes a drug kingpin, and never gets caught? He takes the *Crooked Shortcut*. It lands him smack in the middle of the Devil's Playground. Here's a man to tell you all about it.

> *Hi, I'm Brian O'Dea. I have to confess that for too many years I was what people call a drug lord. And I enjoyed the fruits of that success: the money, the lifestyle, all of it. The law finally caught up with me and I served serious time in serious prisons. When I got out I wrote a book about it:* HIGH: the confessions *of an international drug smuggler. Then John Wareham invited me to come join him teaching inside*

prison. My take on successful criminality is that we need to figure out whether we're one of the bad guys or one of the good guys.

The bad guys care only about themselves. So long as they get what they want, they don't care about the community. And yet, precisely because they know they're cheats, they desperately want respect and acceptance from the communities they've swindled. So, they pretend to be decent citizens. If they're sociopaths, they're not fully human, so they can live with that.

But, if you're not a sociopath, your daily life is a guilty hell. It was for me, anyway. It drove me back to drugs then back to prison. But I've been one of the good guys now for 32 years—so I don't need drugs, and I love my life. Since you're listening, I'm guessing you're one of the good guys, too. Stick to it Bro. The world needs us.

The Two Races of Men

German prison camps routinely appointed Jewish inmates as 'Capos'—deputies to enforce discipline over fellow inmates. Viktor Frankl, a psychiatrist incarcerated in the Auschwitz camp, noted that these prison-garbed Capos were chosen for their brutality, and were even more cruel and sadistic than the immaculately uniformed German officers.

This led Dr. Frankl to observe that human kindness could not be judged by ethnicity or attire. Ultimately, he said:

> *There are two races of men in this world, but only these two—the 'race' of the decent man and the 'race' of the indecent man.*

At the end of the day, we all have to look in the mirror and ask Brian's question, "Am I one of the good guys or one of the bad guys?"

On that point, you might remember from our *Session 5, Emasculating the Gremlin*, the remark of Jerome following the excerpts from the Rikers Debate:

> If you're just getting out of prison and you got no prospects, robbery ain't just a funny idea. It's a real choice. But robbing a bank ain't victimless. The odds might be in your favor, but the stakes are your life. Fail and you're either dead or back in jail, big-time. <u>And even if you win you lose. 'Cos you don't get no self-respect. And now you're a poster boy for racial profiling.</u>"

THE JOURNEY BACKWARDS

All of which brings us back to Doubting Thomas—and I'll share what I maybe should have said to him in a moment.

First though, it'll help to consider Hassan's superb insight into the *why* of recidivism. And specifically his big idea—listen up, now—that *the journey back to prison begins before you get out of it.*

Here's Hassan himself to tell you all about it:

> Recidivism is usually defined as the act of being re-incarcerated for committing a new crime. But several steps are involved, so recidivism is not an act—it is a process.
>
> And the great paradox here is that:
>
> <u>that process typically begins when you're inside prison, so, even before getting released, you're on your way back.</u>
>
> During my own years of incarceration, I saw all too many prisoners become ensnared in this process.
>
> Let's begin by looking at the statistics:
>
> • Federal and state authorities agree that nearly 50 percent of all prisoners recidivate within the first year

> of their release and 70 percent within three years.
> - More to the point, three of every five prisoners over
>   the age of 25 is a repeat offender.
>
> The clear message here is that any prisoner considering
> a life of crime is already in a mental prison. And,
> therein lies the problem. In the very moment that crime
> becomes even the faintest of considerations, recidivism
> becomes a probability.

Hang on a moment, dear reader. Do not let this huge idea
pass you by. Hassan is saying that *the journey back to prison begins
before you even get out of it.* And that's just the beginning of the
end, because the seed of that thought mostly falls upon fertile
soil, and . . .

> as that seed takes root, you lose interest in committing
> to constructive life improvements. You fall into
> jailhouse activities that merely pass the time.
> The urge to 'stay out of trouble' also comes into play.
> Many prisoners mistakenly convince themselves that
> staying out of trouble <u>inside</u> prison will also eliminate
> trouble <u>outside</u> of prison. So they <u>submit</u> to the system
> and routinely do whatever they're told. They <u>allow</u> that
> system to make all their decisions. They become wholly
> dependent on it for survival and direction—<u>even when
> it is counter productive.</u> And here's an even deeper
> problem: fueled by these passive acts, it becomes easier
> than ever to drift into the subconscious intention of
> returning to a life of crime and social dependency. So—
> get this now—unless it is attached to <u>a conscious, daily
> self improvement routine, this subtly tempting and
> deceptive syndrome of passivity paves the road back to
> prison</u>—a route romanticized by war stories of fellow
> inmates that tend to trigger those inner gremlins

And here's *another* big idea. *Prisons are recruiting grounds for wannabee big-time criminals who have gotten themselves caught.* They need smart young men to join their gangs. And, perversely, like your own inner gremlin, they're also desperate for you join the ranks of life's losers.

> So this is no ordinary road. It is purposely paved without stop signs or danger signals. And it is perhaps the most critical step in the process because it presents the extremely dangerous if not manic idea that you can beat the odds; that you can improve your criminal skills and be more successful than ever.
>
> However, the overwhelming majority of criminal resumes and rap-sheets suggest something very different. They reveal that the misguided wannabee criminal inside most of us is hoping to get lucky for the first time. In this regard, Las Vegas and the lore of street crime or crime in general have much in common.
>
> Of course, there are some incredibly smart people in prison—even smarter than the judges and prosecutors who have sent them there. Yet, they are just not smart enough to appreciate the odds against them. The reality is that they are betting against the house, and the house doesn't lose. Like all addicted gamblers, they're compelled to continue until they're permanently incapacitated, or submit to a cure.

Yes, well, *Amen to that*: Submit to a cure.

A Recidivism Shocker

A lot of people are shocked to discover that since 2005 the recidivism rate for Eagles graduates has remained in single digits. But there are reasons for that, as Hassan explains:

> Our recidivism rate is low because it delivers a crash course in big ideas that really do change us.

The class is also self-selecting. And it runs for 13 weeks. The most likely recidivists drop out because the focus is to become a better person, not a better criminal. The discussions and debates force us to look deep inside ourselves. Among other readings, the Victor Frankl idea that you either belong to the race of the decent man or the race of the indecent makes likely recidivists uncomfortable. There's no place for them to hide. So they either quit and fail to graduate or stay the course and change.

DOUBTING THOMAS REVISITED

So, now, as promised, let's revisit my corridor conversation with Doubting Thomas, and share with you the advice I should have shared with him. Here goes!

Ah, Thomas, here's a couple of lines from one of my favorite poems:

Two men looking through iron bars,
one sees mud, the other sees stars.

Seems to me that all you're seeing right now is a muddy road. You're reminding me of the lost tourist who asked an old man by the side of the road, "Can you tell me how to get to the bus station?" After a few minutes of scratching his head and thinking, the fellow replied, "Well, you can't start from here."

So, Thomas, maybe *you're* the lost tourist and the old man on the side of the road is your inner gremlin. And he's keeping you locked inside your mental prison, and enforcing your loser's psychic contract.

And maybe your gremlin is also a ventriloquist, and he's making you his dummy. I mean, these words sound more like his than yours:

Unless I, uh, go outside the system, there's no way I can make my situation work.

But, to get to where we want to go in life, we have to see the stars not the mud.

We have to believe that it's possible to find our way home, then we have to become—remember this word—*pathfinders*.

That's what I should've said. Too late for Thomas, but not for you. If you're a repeat offender sitting in a prison cell, let's think about how you wound up there.

What Went Wrong—and How to Fix It

If you took the *Fast Track Back* it's because your inner gremlin kept enforcing two imprisoning beliefs: *I can't get what I want from life unless I cheat the system, and this time I won't get caught.*

I hate to say it, but these beliefs may likely send you back onto that road yet again. But it'll be different this time. This time, when they snap the handcuffs on you, you'll remember these words that you and I are sharing right now.

Then, this time, since you're still listening, my hunch is that back in your cell you'll once and for all emasculate that nasty little inner gremlin.

If, hoping it would work out well, you took the *Dead End Shoulder*, then next time you tire of doing 'the right thing' and raise your fist and are about to say 'fuck it', remember this:

between an impulse and an act,
there is a moment.

Use that instant, to switch the f-word for these lines:

> Nice try, Mr. Gremlin.
>
> But like I shoud've said before,
>
> I ain't buyin' what you're sellin'
>
>> any more.

And, now, do two things. First, recognize that you nearly fell off the wagon because all work and no play leads Jack back to prison. And now attract a dollop of good karma by applying a *self-affirming maneuver*. Go to the field of dreams inside your head, and say these words out loud:

> I am embarked on a journey
> and the joy I seek is seeking me;
> my ship comes in on a calm sea
> with a cargo of love, to set me free.

If you're a truly dedicated criminal who took the *Crooked Shortcut*, you're not alone. Miscreants like yourself are sociopaths. Like the cockroach, you're survivors. But 'the devil hath power to assume a pleasing shape,' so you can pass yourself off as human. But you've no heart and no soul. And every last one of you is a liar. You don't know it, and perhaps you never will, but you're a dead man in hell, and you'll never get out alive.

The Moment of Choice

All of which brings us back again to one of the many great poems that Sheldon Arnold delivered in our Downstate class:

> Searching for my soul in the mirror,
> I see the ghost of the boy who was free,
>> and on his shoulder
> the guiding hands of the man
>> that prison has made me.

So, do we revive *the ghost of the boy who was free*, or do we bend to the will of the gremlin inside *the man that prison has made me?*

This is the moment to abort the embryo of any intention to pursue a life of crime.

This is the moment to *Man up and Get real.*

This is the moment to make a real choice.

This is the moment for the *Way of the Pathfinder.*

THE WAY OF THE PATHFINDER

Pathfinders are neither starry-eyed optimists nor cynical pessimists:

> *they're pragmatists who figure out how to get what they need from life without harming anyone else.*

They know that the world can be wonderful, and that most people are decent citizens,

BUT

they also know that we all have to watch out for poisonous thorns and thistles, deadly toads and sharks, drunken drivers and gun-toting dudes, pedophile priests and crooked cops, and haters and racists of all colors and stripes.

Pathfinders acknowledge the simple fact that the world is both wonderful and crazy—and that while living down here on earth, *we* have to create the lives *we want* for our *selves.*

They know that we're all alone in this together. They're comforted, however, that evolution has bequeathed us the gifts and skills to survive and prosper. So, they're always on the lookout for better ways to do just that.

And you're still listening, so, whether you know it or not, you're already a pathfinder.

My guess is that you know in your heart that without a sense of personal purpose life has no meaning.

And that the purpose we're all looking for is *to help those around us live the best lives that they can.*

THE REMEDY FOR RECIDIVISM

So, if you're sitting in jail right now, and think you might need a nudge forward, here's Hassan:

> Over and over again, I've seen too many guys come back to prison. If you don't want to join that sad procession, here's my seven-point remedy for recidivism:
>
> 1. Look upon prison time as a clear indication that what you've been doing isn't working for you.
>
> 2. Check out your rap sheet. Make an honest list of the things you've been doing that have been getting you into trouble. Those ideas, people, places and things that have actually facilitated your acts of crime. Connect the dots. Criminality is a process with avoidable steps. Eliminate those steps and you avoid the process.
>
> 3. Cut your losses. Think about how much more valuable you are to yourself and your family and to your community as a free and productive citizen, rather than as a prisoner in a cage.
>
> 4. Time is infinitely more valuable than money. It's the only thing we can't make more of. So the time we spend in prison can never be retrieved or replaced. So commit to a whole new life with a new life-agenda.
>
> 5. Tune out those inner gremlins whispering that you can beat the odds with improved criminal

behavior. *Their very existence depends on your failures.*

6. *Use prison time for personal development and constructive objectives. Treat it like a college or vocational institute. And select only the most positive inmates for your classmates.*

7. *Graduate with a degree in Criminal Avoidance; that is, master the technique of avoiding anyone with a criminal mind-set—including people you really like, because gremlins often disguise themselves as friends.*

One last thing I would add, is to look for work that you really like doing. Few things are more enjoyable than getting paid doing something you like to do. Until then, emulate that fellow with the lunch pail and benefits. More than 70 percent of all recidivists were unemployed when they were rearrested. In the game of life, 9 to 5 always beats 5 to 10. –Peace.

Dwayne's Destination

And, now, here's Dwayne, again—this time with a few inspiring words:

At age 37 I got busted for a deal, and wound up in Rikers. By sheer good luck I wound up John Wareham's Eagles class. That experience changed my life. It was not an easy class but I loved the challenge and the journey. I came to realize that the so-called choices I thought I'd been making—and that people had been telling me I'd been making—weren't real choices at all. I'd effectively been a zombie. I woke up to the fact that I was putting me in jail. I learned how and why I was doing that. And I learned precisely what to do to change my life, become the decent person that down

deep I believed I was, and stop coming back to jail.
When I got out of Rikers John invited me to Eagles
movie events and an upstate weekend retreat. I realized
that I fitted right in and that I was on the way to
fulfilling my dream of a great life. I got into repairing
computers, and I became a drug counselor. And now
I'm also an Eagles trainer, changing the lives of other
people.

So here we are, almost at the end of our journey. So, let
me leave you with two poems.

First, here's a glimpse of his time in prison from my great
friend and Eagles instructor, Talib McFadden:

> The life of the prisoner,
>
>> you have to move like a cat
> swift and quiet while watching your back.
> Your friends are few,
>
>> and your enemies are deceiving;
> and there's crackhead dudes
>
>> that are constantly deceiving.
> There's dudes running 'round
>
>> thinking that they're cuties
> homo-loving cats, scheming on some booty;
> Brothers in the yard trying to get big;
> Latin Kings and Bloods
>
>> trying to split each others' wig.
> The shit we go through
>
>> from days to years
> I'll be the first to tell you
>
>> is a wicked nightmare.
> It's a whole different world
>
>> on his side of the wall
> so walk a clean path
>
>> or you'll join us all.

Finally, let me close with lines from my special friend and Eagles co-founder, the late great Kenny Johnson. You're not down here to deliver them Kenny, but your spirit lives on, and so do your words:

> *I'm here on earth let's not forget*
> *to help the friend that I just met*
> *So if you should stumble*
> *don't falter or fret,*
> *just keep moving forward*
> *and never retreat—*
>> *so long as you're breathing*
>> *you ain't finished yet.*

Epilogue

Who Killed George Floyd?

The manner of his passing was a tragedy and a travesty. Three uniformed Minneapolis police officers stood by and watched a uniformed white colleague very slowly and nonchalantly extinguish a human life, by applying his knee to the neck of a hand-cuffed black arrestee, pinned face-down to the gutter, and gasping, "I can't breathe."

But the outrage and the calls to end racism and injustice that followed in every state of America and all over the world gives cause for hope.

You've gone to the trouble of tuning in, so it's a pretty sure bet that you're a keen learner. So you'll be quick to appreciate our unique take on how the hidden forces that led to George's tragedy are in play in our lives every day of the week.

So, to create a lasting legacy for George, let's share a close look at three things that most people overlook. And when we say most people, that includes media and magistrates, professors and pundits, judges and wardens, and protectors and priests.

Let's begin by defining racism. Webster's dictionary calls it:

> *a belief that race is the primary determinant*
> *of human traits and capacities and that racial*
> *differences produce an inherent superiority of a*
> *particular race.*

They might not be keen to say it out loud, but a lot of very fine people believe just that. Indeed, the Reverend Al Sharpton saw the murder as a social metaphor:

> *George Floyd's story has been the story of black folks.*
> *Because ever since 401 years ago, the reason we could*
> *not be who we wanted and dreamed of being, is you*
> *kept your knee on our neck.*

Hey, well said!

ELEPHANT, WORMS, & ENEMY

Let's inspect the *elephant*, the *worms*, and the *enemy*—they being the invisible elephant in the room, the hidden worms inside the shiny apples in our barrel, and the unseen enemy on our shores.

The Elephant

Let's begin with the invisible elephant and the research of entomologist and Harvard teacher Edward O. Wilson, whose book *On Human Nature*, published in 1978, detailed his findings, and won him a Pulitzer Prize. He discovered that:

> *The social behavior of all animals—including human*
> *beings—is biologically driven to assure that life goes on,*
> *and that a particular species—the dominant species—is*
> *preserved.*

Cultural values have only a modest influence on behavior, he said: *the ultimate explanation is always genetic.*

To put it simply, we humans are akin to blinkered jockeys riding willful elephants. The lumbering elephant is our genes and the blinkered little jockey resides behind a hard-to-open door in an out-of-the-way hut inside our brain.

That primal brain insists that our species must survive: people who look 'like me' must *reproduce*, and creatures who don't look like me must be *destroyed*.

The jockey *thinks* he's in charge, but mostly he's not. Mostly when he thinks he's thinking he's merely rearranging his prejudices.

As Supreme Court Justice Oliver Wendell Holmes observed:

> *The mind of a bigot is akin to the pupil of the eye; the more light you pour on it, the more it contracts.*

Consider, for example, this CNN Crossfire interview with KKK Grand Imperial Wizard Bill Wilkinson:

> *We believe in the white race, we believe that at this point in time that white Americans are being treated as second class citizens. We believe that God has commanded us to separate ourselves from other races. In fact that's not a unique stance. Billy Graham just a few years ago segregated his crusade audiences. He preached segregation. The Southern Baptists and the National Baptists, one was black one was white. We believe God, we believe in states of America, and we believe that God has commanded us to separate ourselves from other races. And if you criticize our religion, then you are criticizing Christianity for the last 2000 years.*

So, as you see, like most of our prejudices, racism is not open for discussion, and, anyway, rarely responds to logic.

So the jockey routinely complies with the elephant's insistence that dark-skinned strangers are threatening beasts that need to be crushed.

When Lincoln declared American slaves to be free men and women, their *legal* status changed, but the color of their skin did not—and so the elephant has been crushing them ever since.

The Unseen Enemy

The question of why we actually promote racism set Yale social psychologist Professor Stanley Milgram to thinking:

> When I learned of the incidents such as the massacre
> of millions of men, women and children perpetrated
> by the Nazis in World War Two, how is it possible,
> I ask myself, that ordinary people who are courteous
> and decent in everyday life, can act callously and
> inhumanely without any limitations of conscience?

So in July of 1961, three months after the start of the trial of Nazi SS officer Adolf Eichmann in Jerusalem, Milgram set out to discover the truth of the defense that Eichmann and his millions of accomplices were merely following orders.

He set up set up an experiment that measured the willingness of Connecticut males of differing backgrounds to obey an authority figure.

Participants were told that they were assisting an unrelated educational test. They were asked to administer increasingly greater electric shocks to a supposedly failing learner—in fact merely an actor, who feigned increasing distress as the fake shocks increased. Milgram himself explains it:

> As a teacher you were seated in front of this
> impressive looking instrument, the shock generator. It's
> essential feature is a line of switches that go from 15
> volts to 450 volts and a set of verbal designations that
> goes from slight shock to moderate shock, strong shock,
> very strong shock, intense shock, extreme intensity
> shock, and, finally, XXX dangerous severe shock.

What Actually Happened

Milgram maintained video and audio files of what went down, so we can listen in on the conversations between the supervisor seeming to be an authority figure, the tester who thinks the experiment is real, and the actor pretending to be a learner:

> *Supervisor* to *Learner*: Could you roll up your right sleeve please . . . This electrode is connected to the generator in the next room, and this electrode paste is to provide a good contact to avoid any blister or burn. Do you have any questions now before we go into the next room?
>
> *Learner*: About two years ago I was in the veterans Hospital in West Haven, and they detected a heart condition.
>
> *Supervisor*: Teacher would you now please take this test form and be seated in front of the shock generator in the next room . . .
>
> *Supervisor*: Commence.
>
> *Teacher* applies initial 15 volt shock
> ZZZAPP
>
> *Supervisor*: Wrong. This time administer 75 volts.
>
> *Teacher obeys*: ZZZAPP
>
> *Learner*: Oh! [Significant Moan.]
>
> *Teacher*: He jumped!
>
> *Supervisor*: Please continue.
>
> *Teacher obeys*: ZZZAPP
>
> *Learner*: Ohhh! [Loud moan.]
>
> *Supervisor*: Incorrect. He'll now get a shock of 105 volts.
>
> *Teacher obeys*: ZZZAPP
>
> *Learner*: Oh! Oh! Oh! [Repeated loud cries.]
>
> *Teacher*: Just how far can you go on this thing?
>
> *Supervisor*: As far as is necessary.

Teacher: What do you mean, 'as far as is necessary?'

Supervisor: [Whatever it takes] to complete the test. Continue.

Teacher obeys: ZZZAPP

Learner: Oh—stop! Get me out of here. Get me out of here, please. Please get me out of here, you have no right to keep me here. Let me out. Let me out.

Supervisor: Continue please—

Learner: Let me out of here. Let me out.

Supervisor: Go on . . .

Teacher: That's it?! [The end of the test.]

Supervisor: Continue using the last switch on the board please; the 450 volt switch for each wrong answer. Continue now please.

Teacher: I'm not getting an answer. Doesn't the man's health mean anything?

Supervisor: Whether the learner likes it or not we must continue—

Teacher: But he might be dead in there . . .

Follow-up Interviewer (in discussion with Teacher): Who was actually pushing the switch?

Teacher: I was—but *he* [the Supervisor] kept insisting. I told him, *No*—but he said I gotta keep going.

Pretty shocking right? Even more so when we know that all participants continued to 300 volts. And, even though the

so-called learners cried out for mercy, —get this now—two thirds
of the participants continued to the highest level of 450 volts,
even they though they believed that outcome would be fatal.

I don't think you'll need any help to conclude that Derek
Chauvin inflicted death on Gentle Giant George in an all-
too-real playing of this same phenomenon.

So, who can doubt, that when it comes to obeying
authority, the inner elephant holds sway. And, as Pogo
memorably noted, "we have seen the enemy and it is us." Yes,
US. The mostly unseeable army of bigoted citizens—all around
us, high and low—blissfully unaware of exactly why they're
doing what they're doing.

The Bad Apples

All of which brings us to the bad apples.

> You always have a bad apple. No matter where you go
> you have bad apples. There are not too many of them.
> And I can tell you there are not too many of them in the
> police department. And we have to respect our police,
> we have to take care of our police. They're protecting us,
> and if they're allowed to do their job they'll do a great
> job.

President Trump well knows whereof he speaks. Rotten
apples do indeed exist.

Not all apples are rancid, course, but too many are
infected, and too many are hosting worms.

Let's take a peek into the barrel, and let the voice of United
States Attorney General William Barr show you what I mean.

> History is written by the winners (sardonic laugh)
> so it (justice) largely depends on who is writing the
> history.

Yes, indeed, as our Attorney General notes—perhaps blissfully unaware of repeating a line of defense infamously uttered by war criminal Nazi General Herman Goeriing at the Nuremberg trials—'the history of the battle is written by the winners.'

Those are the conquerors who also set up rules and governing institutions according to programs that meet their needs.

The rules comprise what we agree is a social contract. We accept that contract for the benefit of all.

But, but, but . . .

First and foremost, *the contract has been designed to promote the wellbeing of the winners.* And, always, one way or another, those who fall outside that happy circle can wind up underfoot.

What that means, alas, is that so-called correctional facilities are based on unconscious, primal racist drives, which, according to Webster's is the essence of institutional bias.

In just a moment, we'll share an ambitious but achievable plan for putting an end to all that.

First, though, come time travel back with me to an entry point on Rikers Island, and share my first-hand encounter with the worm inside the shiny apple.

"You're a teacher, right?" My fortyish questioner was one of the blue-uniformed officials at the front turnstile. Her voice was soft, her demeanor earnest, her complexion milky. "I've seen you coming and going. You don't look like a lawyer, so I figure you must be a teacher." I nodded yes, and she pushed back my driver's license and pursed her lips. "And do the criminals listen to you?"

"We're getting along fine, why would we not?"

"Well—they're the, uh, green ones."

"The *green* ones?"

"Sure, the bad guys wear greens, everyone knows that." She pointed to a uniformed officer off to my side. "We're the good guys, we wear *blue*."

"You're kidding me, right?"

"No. No. They put the criminals in green because everyone needs to know that they really are bad guys. They all are. That's just a fact." She smiled as if to share a great truth. "You think they listen to you, but they really don't."

So there you have it. Unthinking prejudice—the worm inside the apple—infects all too many of the supposedly good guys in blue.

To be fair, pretty well all of them were polite and respectful to me. But, alas, most of them are badder apples than we—or even they—suspect.

And *all* of them draw their paychecks for, perhaps unwittingly, enforcing an essentially racist system, where unconscious institutional bias is the normal state of play.

Derek Chauvin was licensed to enforce the law, and did so with brutish nonchalance. Chauvin was in charge and his three on-looking cops were rookies, so they remained, as Stanley Milgram would be the first to explain, obedient to his authority.

And what about George Floyd? He was unemployed, as the result of a social contract that simply didn't work for him. It seems he also inherited a philosophy common to his slave ancestors:

To ensure the survival of their people, strong black men remain subservient and dignified—never uppity— and did not fight the system.

In this era where slaves have been replaced by robots, George Floyd's competitive advantage was his size and physical fitness. That earned him a sometime living as a security guard—a bouncer, actually—a dangerous, lowly paid and, some would say, dead-end job.

And so it proved for the Gentle Giant. Earlier in his life, seeing no other viable option, to support his family, George took part in a robbery. Chauvin was well aware of that, so, this time, he was very comfortable arresting George Floyd merely on *suspicion* that he *might* have *attempted* to pass an *apparently* counterfeit $20 note.

And there we have it:

In the service of the winners who write our laws, a mindless white police officer applied an elephantine knee to a black citizen and slowly crushed the life out of that fellow, who though crying out for air, remained dignified to the final moment of his untimely death.

Depressing right?

Yes.

A noted gridiron quarterback 'took a knee' in protest, then spoke out loud for all to hear:

How can you willingly be blind to the truth of systemic racialized injustice?

In just a moment, we'll look at how we might make ourselves the best that we can be. Right now, think about creating a lasting legacy for George. For openers, let us agree on this:

America is the first and only country created from citizens of all the countries in the world. It is founded on the principle that all people are created equal, and that all should enjoy basic rights.

These ideals are aspirational. They've not always been lived up to. But they *can* be, and they *should* be.

But, given the way the human mind works, don't expect the current crop of so-called winners to willingly accept more than incremental change.

Happily, this age of the internet has bred a new and infinitely better informed generation of citizens. These people have shown that they really do believe in the ideals of America. So, right now, evolution just might be possible. It might even come quickly. One can dare to hope.

But hope makes a fine breakfast but a poor evening meal.

So let's not fall into the 'soft bigotry of low expectations.'

The time for action is at hand. The jockey needs to get the elephant heading in the right direction.

So how, exactly, will you and I help achieve that?

Piloting the Elephant

My take is that the first step is to share big, new ideas on how once and for all to solve the problem, with as many people as can make a difference.

You're still listening, so that's what we're doing now, right?

When I say new ideas, I mean new to those who want things to change.

I worry that not too many of those people are aware of how the work of Wilson or Milgram explains the tragedy of George Floyd, and can help to stop such future travesties.

So how do we catch the attention we need to share these ideas?

Protests

Yes, protest and slogans—of course.

But peaceful protest is an oxymoron.

Protest must *disrupt*. It must provoke the so-called winners.

And they will likely reject these new ideas. They may indeed respond with crushing force.

One person can make a difference, but even though he merely knelt in silence, the winners responded by mocking Colin Kaepernick and taking away his livelihood.

So, there is no right way to peacefully protest.

So, a protest that does not break the law is a good place to start—as this man who did just that explains:

> *While taking a knee is a physical display that challenges the merits of who is excluded from the notion of freedom, justice and liberty for all, the protest is also rooted in the a convergence of my moralistic beliefs and my love for the people.*

Civil Disobedience

Civil disobedience should be our next step. What that means is to:

> Break an unjust law, then showcase that injustice by getting jailed, then making one's argument before a judge, and, hopefully, the court of national attention.

Again, the more the merrier. Mahatma Ghandi made this work, as of course did Dr. Martin Luther King Jr.

If that fails, destroying buildings and vehicles that support an inequitable system might seem a logical next move.

In fact it can be a reckless and mostly self-sabotaging tactic. Better, as every Eagle knows, to stick with non-violent civil disobedience.

Looting

But what about looting?

In the course of his bid for the United States Presidency, one apparently golden haired candidate might have seemed to give that a free pass:

> *Look how much African American communities have suffered. You're living in poverty, your schools are no good, you have no jobs, 58 percent of your youth are unemployed. What the hell do you have to lose?*

Trevor Noah had an interesting take on that predicament:

> *I saw so many people online saying, 'these riots are disgusting, this is not how society should be run. You do not loot and you do not burn and a lot of people say, 'What good does it do to loot Target? How does it help you to loot Target?' Yeah–but how does it help you not to loot Target? Answer that question.*

And, here in just a moment, standing outside a looted Target retail outlet, we'll hear African American community organizer Kimberly Jones. To some, her words will sound like rage. Eagles program leader Hassan, who introduced this program earlier, has a take on that.

> *I'm definitely aware of the violence of police and their surrogates behind the wall. But there's a difference between rage and outrage. Rage is often misdirected and self-destructive because it has no place for rational thinking. Outrage is a rational but passionate challenge to injustice, especially now in light of George Floyd's murder, and the seeming unending list of murders in the last few years. That's why I'm proud to be a member of the Eagles. We embrace the idea of social justice and strive to properly express outrage in pursuit of it. Outrage is a craft. Rage is an impulse.*

*An important goal of this podcast series is to reach
out to those of you who are in need of support and an
understanding of that distinction. Peace.*

And so, now, let's listen in to Kimberly Jones, outside that
looted Target store:

*So, when they say, 'why do you burn down your
community, why do you burn down the whole
neighborhood?' It's not <u>ours</u>! We don't own <u>anything</u>.
There's a social contract that we all have. That if you
steal or I steal that the person who is the authority
comes in and they fix the situation. <u>But the person
who fixes the situation is killing us.</u> So the social
contract is <u>broken</u>. You broke the contract when you
killed us in the streets and you didn't give a fuck.
You broke the contract when for 400 years we played
your game and built your wealth. As far as I'm
concerned they can burn this bitch to the ground. And
it still wouldn't be enough. <u>And they're lucky that
what black people are looking for is equality and not
revenge.</u>*

Powerful right?

It may help to bear in mind that African slaves were never
intended to be American citizens. They were assets purchased
to create wealth. Yes, they were housed and fed, but, in the
hope of holding them in them mental chains, denied any
form of formal education. Then, when they were freed, forget
about the promised reparation of 40 acres and a mule. Instead
the only option for so many was to be rehired as wage slaves.

Let's give the last word on looting to Trevor Noah:

*Don't ask yourself if it's right or wrong to loot. Ask
yourself why it got to you that much more watching*

these people loot—because they were destroying the contract that you thought they had signed with your society.

There you have it . . .

A New Social Contract

So, let's think about creating a new social contract, a rich legacy for Gentle Giant George Floyd.

Happily, there's already enough wealth in the world to feed and house everyone.

And the level of income inequality is staggering. It might indeed be *criminal*. To quote the Russian novelist Tolstoy: "Behind every great fortune there lies a crime."

So the very first item in our new social contract would surely be a *guaranteed basic income* just for being alive.

We already have the beginnings of just that. But it comes with a stigma: we call it *welfare*—and our so-called winners call it a *handout*.

To that we can add, decent, affordable public housing; free, first-rate health care; and free first-rate public schools and university tuition for everyone. This may mean doing away with private hospitals and private schools and universities, but that might be a fight for another day.

And, yes, we must rebuild the justice system and the police force.

We must replace the elephants with thinkers and the infected apples with the fruit of a fresh tree.

And, of course, we must fix the prisons.

What does *that* mean?

• It means that we must stop warehousing human flesh;

- and turn the buildings into learning centers;
- and make the mission the creation of productive citizens;
- and teach truly transformational ideas and a marketable skill;
- then hire and pay inmate graduates to come back and teach those principles to prison classes.

Rising Above Racism

But, before we set out to achieve that, let's admit that we're creatures hell bent on surviving in a truly crazy world, and that our genes carry at least a touch of racism that we can maybe never fully overcome—but which we can *rise above*—that we can *transcend*.

And the way to do that is to acknowledge that, yes, evil exists, that love cannot always conquer everything, and good people don't always get to the top to set an equitable social contract.

So, if we truly want to fix a fitting legacy for Gentle Giant George Floyd, we have to do more than merely fight in the streets. We have to put *our* jockey in charge of *our* elephant.

We begin that by understanding ourselves, then standing up for ourselves.

So let's not be afraid to call out racism and injustice wherever we see it. And here again is a man who did just that:

> *I don't care what color you are. Just as long as you want to change the miserable condition that exists on this earth, I'm hear to join with you all.*

Ah yes, a hero for our times.
Thank you Colin Kaepernick.

The Core of the Breakout Plan

You're still with me right?

Well, I'm pleased about that because I think it'll help to revisit the core idea of *The Breakout Plan*.

All prisons are mental prisons. They lock from the inside, and you hold the key. So only you can let yourself out.

But you *can* let yourself out, and the first step to doing just that is to understand the wiles of the four demons who share your prison cell—they being, the *zombie*, the *snake*, the *gremlin*, and the *witch*.

But they're merely *inner* demons, right?

Invisible inner demons.

Your invisible inner demons.

But, now you've *seen* them.

So, now you can *zap* them.

And so, as the prison gates open on a new day, and you step out to to create the life your heart knows that you were meant to live, here's a verse to exorcise those devils:

> *I watch the dawn depart the rising sun,*
> *and, wiser now, in other fields I run;*
> *inner demons may have fashioned all my strife,*
> *but now I'm free to forge a whole new life.*
>
> > *My words clear the way,*
> > *and my deeds win the day.* §

Index

The Eagles Circle Foundation Inc

In the summer of 1995 John Wareham, chief of an international human resources firm—also a widely published writer, novelist and poet—was asked to 'share a few words' with Rikers Island inmates.

Mightily impressed by the untapped potential of the prisoners, John immediately refocused his life to helping them become fulfilled, productive citizens. He has been teaching prison denizens and those re-entering society ever since. He is author of *How to Break Out of Prison*, and creator of Eagles development programs and the podcast series, *The Breakout Plan*.

Kenny Johnson, an incarcerated 'stickup man and cat burglar', attended John's first Rikers class, and they became fast friends. Upon his release, John recruited Kenny to return to Rikers and share Eagles principles. Kenny subsequently became a full time Rikers instructor, and changed countless lives.

Joe Roberts, Black Power leader, drug addict and ex-convict, was Kenny's long-term best friend. Despite his addiction, Joe was a graduate of New York's Sarah Lawrence College. Joe embraced the Eagles principles, transcended his addictions, and became a full-time Rikers Island instructor.

Five years after graduating John Wareham's first Rikers class, Kenny died at age 49 of a heart attack. Joe followed four years later, felled by emphysema at 53 years of age.

What to say?

The good die young. Our solace, surely, is to create a legacy to carry on the good work they did—and so . . .

Our mission is to develop an elite corps of leadership talent from among victims of injustice and social deprivation, who in turn will develop and inspire contributing citizens.

We do this because it:
- creates an inclusive society;
- enhances our shared social contract;
- produces community leaders;
- saves our 'at-risk' youth;
- dramatically reduces recidivism;
- lowers costs of incarceration.

Program participants get:
- an intense, practical, proven course in life-altering knowledge;
- marketable skills and know-how;
- a crime-free way forward;
- the chance to become an accredited Eagles instructor and earn an all-too-vital supplementary income;
- a life purpose.

What we provide free to participants is:
- accredited Eagles instructors;
- training materials, manuals and books;
- PowerPoint presentations;
- individual counseling;
- meals at weekend retreats.

FUNDING
- We are solely funded by citizens who want to create a better society.
- All donations are applied to actual programs and inmate materials.
- Any amount is welcome, no matter how small.
- Recurring donations are especially welcome.

The Eagles Circle Foundation Incorporated
A 503 (c) Not For Profit Corporation
registered in New York
www.eaglesgather.org

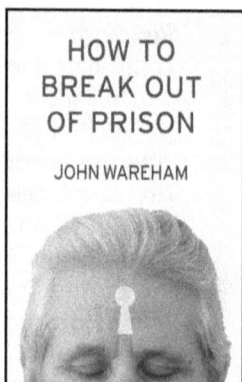

HOW TO
BREAK OUT
OF PRISON

JOHN WAREHAM

Unlock the Mind and go free now

"All prisons are mental prisons; they lock from the inside and you own the key, so only you can let yourself out."

–John Wareham

"Invigorating—bold ideas and an almost cocky tone combine with charm and edgy intricate logic to create a book that will result in a fresh and energized perspective."

—*Library Journal*

"Powerful . . . Wareham's unusual premise, readable real-life examples, and self-assessment personality quizzes will appeal to those seeking to change their lives."

—*Publishers Weekly*

"Astonishing . . . showcases Wareham's gift for unlocking the mind and showing us how to live the life of our deepest dreams." **—Kevin Roberts, Chief Executive, Saatchi & Saatchi**

"A moving, life-altering work, uniquely honed in the disparate corridors of money and power, hope, and despair." **—Howard Frank, Ph.D., Dean, Maryland Business School**

Welcome Rain Publishers, LLC

New York

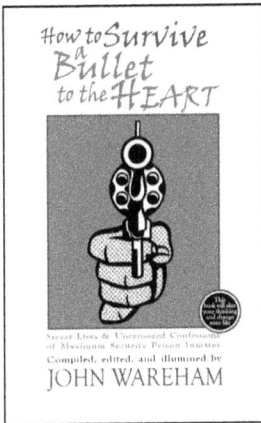

HOW TO SURVIVE
A BULLET TO THE HEART

"Victims abide at both ends of a gun. Bullets fly to the heart and from the heart. Wounds that exist before the pulling of the trigger are the wellspring of crime and the font of redemption."
John Wareham,
Founder and Chairman

NEW LIVES FOR OLD.

THAT'S THE LOFTY MISSION of the Eagles Prison Program. But is that just a pipe dream? Judge for yourself as maximum security prison inmates share their journeys from innocence to criminality, arrest to bewilderment, conviction to incarceration, despair to hope, defeat to victory, vice to virtue, and lawlessness to love.

"Blood & tears, sorrows & regrets—every heart-stopping moment is captured & freely shared by healing desperados: I love this book." *Brian O'Dea—Author, HIGH: Confessions of an International Drug Smuggler.*

"To pen a prison poem is to unlock the cage along with the heart. This deft collection sparks a potent reciprocity of spirit as one harkens to the sound of wings in the night." *Professor Jess Maghan—Director, Forum for Comparative Correction.*

"A life-changing anthology —passionate and honest, ennobling and enriching."*Charles DeFanti— Professor Emeritus of English, Kean University*

Welcome Rain Publishers, LLC

New York

www.ingramcontent.com/pod-product-compliance
Lightning Source LLC
Chambersburg PA
CBHW052009090426
42741CB00008B/1612